D0690491

FLAGSTAFF
PAST & PRESENT

By RICHARD & SHERRY MANGUM

Foreword by BRUCE BABBITT

NORTHLAND PUBLISHING

*To those pioneers
who made Flagstaff
a special place.*

*A special thanks goes to James E. Babbitt
for his generous help and encouragement.*

Text © 2003
by Richard K. Mangum and Sherry G. Mangum, Authors are trustors and
beneficiaries of their family trust by terms of trust agreement.

All rights reserved.

This book may not be reproduced in whole or in part, by any means
(with the exception of short quotes for the purpose of review), without permission of the publisher. For information, address Permissions, Northland
Publishing, 2900 North Fort Valley Road, Flagstaff, Arizona 86001.

www.northlandpub.com

Composed in the United States of America
Printed in Hong Kong

Edited by Tammy Gales
Designed by David Jenney
Production supervised by Donna Boyd

FIRST IMPRESSION 2003

ISBN 0-87358-829-0 (hardcover)
04 05 06 07   5 4 3 2

ISBN 0-87358-847-9 (softcover)
04 05 06 07   5 4 3 2

Library of Congress Cataloging-in-Publication Data

Mangum, Richard K.
Flagstaff : past & present / by Richard and Sherry Mangum.
p. cm.
1. Flagstaff (Ariz.)—History—Pictorial works.
2. Flagstaff (Ariz.)—Pictorial works.
3. Historic sites—Arizona—Flagstaff—Pictorial works.
4. Flagstaff (Ariz.)—Buildings,
structures, etc.—Pictorial works. I. Mangum, Sherry G. II. Title.

F819.F57M36 2003

979.1'33—dc21   2003046481

FRONTISPIECE: *This historic 1902 photo provides a unique glimpse into Flagstaff's past. It was taken from the railroad section house, where laundry was often seen fluttering on a clothesline. The prominent businesses seen north of the tracks are the Bank Hotel, Pulliam and Vail Gent's Furnishings, two saloons, two cafés, the Commercial Hotel, a saloon/liquor store, and another café. Hidden by the section house roof are a barber shop, a café, and two more saloons. It's no wonder why the block was called Whiskey Row.*

OPPOSITE: *Hose carts were Flagstaff's original fire engines. Horses would panic around a fire, so the carts were pulled by men. The first team to the scene was paid, so hose cart racing began as a training exercise. The Milton team, shown here, won the Fourth of July competition in 1905.*

All photographs courtesy of Richard and Sherry Mangum unless stated below.

The Following Photography © 2003 by:

Tom Alexander: 38 (bottom right), 55 (right), 69 (bottom), 98, 103 (left)
Peter Bloomer: 5, 46, 76, 77 (left), 86, 88, 89, 95
Michael Collier: 61, 64 (top right), 65 (top)
Tim Gales: 80
Klaus Kranz: 65 (bottom left), 85 (top right)
Sherry Mangum: 12 (bottom), 27 (top right), 29, 34 (bottom right), 35 (top), 53 (right), 59 (top), 62, 64 (bottom right), 65 (bottom right), 74 (middle), 78, 82 (top), 88-89 (background), 91, 99, 100, 102 (top), 104 (bottom left and bottom right), 105 (bottom)
Robert McDonald: Cover (top), 64 (top left and bottom left), 101
John Running: 79, 103 (right)
Jill Torrance: 108
Courtesy of Arizona Historical Society: Cover (bottom), v, 13 (top), 16 (left), 19, 22-23, 30, 31, 32 (top left), 34 (left and top right), 38 (top right), 41, 45, 56, 57 (top), 58, 59 (bottom), 66-67 (left), 72 (bottom), 87 (bottom), 105 (top)
Courtesy of Arizona Office of Tourism: 75
Courtesy of The Arizona Republic: 97
Courtesy of Arizona State Archives: 17 (bottom), 44, 81, 96 (top right)
Courtesy of James Babbitt: 12 (top), 26, 27 (bottom)
Courtesy of James Babbitt, photograph by Earle Forrest: 21
Courtesy of Fronske Collection: 92
Courtesy of W. L. Gore: 90
Courtesy of Grand Canyon National Park, Vogelsang Collection: 32-33 (right)
Courtesy of Phyllis Hogan: 102 (bottom)
Courtesy of the Inn at 410: 107
Courtesy of Lake County (IL) Discovery Museum, Curt Teich Postcard Archives: 70, 72 (top)
Courtesy of the Monte Vista Hotel, photograph by Peter Bloomer: 73
Courtesy of Museum of New Mexico Palace of the Governors: 8-9
Courtesy of Museum of Northern Arizona: x, 15, 20 (top), 24, 28, 36-37, 39, 40
Courtesy of Northern Arizona University, Special Collections and Archives: ii-iii, ix, 6, 10, 11, 14, 16 (right), 17 (top), 20 (bottom), 25, 27 (top left and top middle), 32 (bottom left), 42, 43, 47, 48 (right), 52, 53 (left), 54, 57 (bottom), 63, 67 (right), 68, 69 (top), 74 (left and right), 82 (bottom), 83 (left and bottom right), 84, 85 (bottom left), 93, 94, 104 (top right), 106
Courtesy of Photofest: 60
Courtesy of Riordan Mansion State Historic Park: 18
Courtesy of Adrienne Rose: 87 (top)
Courtesy of Sharlot Hall Museum: 13 (bottom)
Courtesy of Earl Slipher, Jr.: 104 (top left)
Courtesy of USGS: 49, 50, 51
Courtesy of Richard Weston: Author Photo

All Rights Reserved.

CONTENTS

FOREWORD

NYONE WHO HAS EVER DRIVEN ACROSS THE desert Southwest winding along old Highway 66 or speeding through on modern Interstate 40 always seems to retain an indelible memory of Flagstaff. Coming west from Albuquerque you cross a monotone plain speckled with saltbush and bunch grass until, leaving Winslow, the snow capped summits of the San Francisco Peaks appear, floating on the far horizon. And then another hour and you are in Flagstaff surrounded by pine forests at the base of a towering blue mountain.

Coming up toward the mountain from any other direction, whether from Phoenix down in the Sonoran Desert, from the west through the inferno of the Mohave Desert, or across the Painted Desert from the north, the experience is much the same. I am home at last, back in a high mountain oasis, sheltered by the sacred mountain.

And when I am away, the memory remains, whatever the season, whether it's snow in the winter, the cool pon-derosa scented summer, the cumulus clouds building over the peaks to an afternoon shower, fields of sunflowers, or aspens turning golden on mountain slopes. Flagstaff is the one place in the thousand-mile stretch from Albuquerque to Los Angeles that no one seems to forget.

Flagstaff did not get off to an organized start. For whatever reason, the place that would become our town was not in the original plan—the grading and track laying gangs pushed right past the mountain, hardly stopping, oblivious to future possibilities. And

The County Courthouse is a prominent landmark in this photo of town taken from Cherry Hill around 1904.

all those carefully located railroad towns like Gallup, Winslow, Williams, Ash Fork, Kingman, Needles, and Barstow have languished in the byways of history while Flagstaff spontaneously took root to grow into the thriving city that we know today.

Flagstaff was, as the real estate developers say, about location, location, location. The first determinant was the forest—the giant ponderosas, good yellow pine, and easy accessibility. By 1900, Flagstaff was the biggest sawmill complex in the west, sawing several hundred million board-feet of timber each year.

Today, the timber industry is gone, the victim of years of excess cutting. The big mills, located at either end of the town have been torn down and replaced by car dealerships and warehouses. The authors capture that bygone era in the striking photographs—train loads of huge, hand-sawed logs, workers cutting ties at the old Arizona Lumber and Timber mill, and the Riordan mansions which still stand on a small knoll surrounded by shopping centers and university dormitories.

Flagstaff, however, did not just fold up and fade away like McNary in the White Mountains and so many other once prosperous mill towns. Location was still working in its favor. Out around the mountain in the Pueblo towns on the mesas, the Hopi clans continued their traditional way of life, their beautiful and profound ceremonials drawing artists, anthropologists, and tourists from around the world. Nearby, the Navajo, following their flocks across the painted deserts, evoked similar interest and admiration, and Flagstaff grew into a southwestern Samarkand, a crossroads where cultures intersected, intermingled, and traded their arts and crafts.

It was also the location that attracted scientists and their enterprises. It began with John Wesley Powell and the Grand Canyon; others soon followed. Percival Lowell came seeking clear skies for his observatory, Harold Colton to probe the archaeological secrets of the ancient Indian ruins, and others to study the volcanoes and their lava fields. Then the United States Geological Survey arrived, finding Flagstaff the perfect place to merge volcanic geology and astronomy into a program of lunar and planetary research. Today, Flagstaff continues as the center of environmental research for the Colorado Plateau.

The text and photographs in this book remind us just how much of the past still survives, not only in the streets of the historic town, but in buildings and sites as disparate as the university campus, the grounds of Lowell Observatory, and the Museum of Northern Arizona. Walking the streets of the historic town or just looking out from the balcony of the Weatherford Hotel provides wonderful insights into the daily life of the merchants, saloon keepers, and hotel owners who came here first. We owe a big debt of gratitude, not only to the original builders, but also to the dedicated preservationists who came along in the nick of time to capture it all. It is an instructive contrast to Phoenix and Tucson, where the past has been largely obliterated by urban renewal and uncontrolled development.

The photographs reveal another interesting fact; the restored historic downtown actually looks more authentic today than it did back in the 1950s, when merchants were "modernizing" by covering the fine old masonry with aluminum siding and plaster. The history that emerges from this fascinating book should encourage us to think carefully about how the past informs the future and about our continuing obligation to protect and nourish the history of our town.

What is now shaping the future of Flagstaff is still another fact of geography—our proximity to more than three million people down in the Salt River Valley. Flagstaff is fast becoming a satellite city, a recreational community of weekend residents from Phoenix and other Valley cities. And over time, that fact may change the character of our town more than anything since E. E. Ayer first arrived in 1882 to build a simple sawmill. ✦

—BRUCE BABBITT
*Former Governor of Arizona
and Secretary of the Interior*

The C. J. Babbitt home on the southeast corner of Beaver and Cherry was considered one of the town's finest when it was finished in 1901. Unfortunately, it was destroyed by fire in the 1960s.

INTRODUCTION

❋

F LAGSTAFF IS A CHARMING LITTLE mountain town nestled below the San Francisco Peaks. Its scenic location has always made it an appealing place to live. However, the history of the earliest inhabitants of the Flagstaff area is still a puzzle. Archaeological evidence suggests that there were people living in this region thousands of years ago, but unfortunately, little is known of their existence. Current knowledge of this area starts a few centuries later with the Sinagua, a people who built communities and lived around northern Arizona for approximately six hundred years, starting around A. D. 700. The name "Sinagua" is Spanish, meaning "without water," and was bestowed on the Sinagua by anthropologists because of their ability to live in the arid region. The Sinagua, who are believed to be ancestors of the Hopi people, left the Flagstaff area around A.D. 1260.

A few years after Columbus arrived in America, Spanish explorers entered the Southwest and annexed huge sections of the New World, including the region around present-day Flagstaff. The seat of power for the Spanish Crown was in Mexico City thousands of miles away, but the Spaniards, driven by their search for gold, sent explorers throughout the region. Coronado led the first party north in 1540, seeking the Seven Cities of Gold. After months of futile hardship, Coronado's men straggled back into Mexico City to report that there were measureless reaches of terrain in the lands that they had crossed, but none of the precious yellow metal. His failure to find these fabled cities did not end Spanish exploration, and several other groups ventured north, including the 1629 group of Franciscan friars, who established a mission on the Hopi mesas. Looking towards the south, these churchmen saw a set of magnificent mountain peaks, which they named for their patron saint, Francis of Assisi. In Spanish, Saint Francis is San Francisco, and the mountains they saw became the San Francisco Peaks.

In 1821, Mexico finally won its independence from Spain and Arizona became Mexican territory. Then, in 1846, the United States and Mexico began a war that lasted approximately two years. Through this conflagration, the victorious United States acquired a huge tract that included New Mexico Territory, which at that time embraced all of modern New Mexico and Arizona. This uncharted territory held vast resources and beauty, and in time, it would encompass a peaceful little mountain town—Flagstaff. ❋

OPPOSITE: *This 1917 photo shows the entire Flagstaff post office staff—a clerk and two mail carriers—standing proudly before their new headquarters at 108 N. San Francisco Street.*

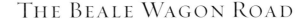

THE BEALE WAGON ROAD

I N 1851, CAPTAIN LORENZO SITGREAVES LED the first United States government expedition across the uncharted New Mexico territory. His main mission was to survey a road across northern Arizona leading into California. The men started from Zuni, New Mexico, and worked their way westward to the Colorado River. In 1853, Francis X. Aubry surveyed the same territory running in the other direction, from California to Albuquerque, looking for a railroad route. And later that same year came Lieutenant Amiel W. Whipple, who was also assigned the task of laying out a railroad route. All of these explorers agreed that northern Arizona provided an excellent natural corridor for a passageway to California.

The job of actually constructing a road fell to Edward F. Beale, an experienced frontiersman and ex-naval officer. Beale was given three tasks: to build a wagon road, to take an inventory of the natural assets of the country, and to test camels as pack animals. Beale left Zuni in 1857, and roughly following the paths of Sitgreaves and Whipple, scratched out a road following the Little Colorado River Valley as far as today's town of Leupp. He then turned toward Flagstaff and reached the Colorado River in about six weeks. Beale was enthusiastic about everything he found. He reported that the route was a good one, there was plentiful grass and water for a livestock industry, an immense pine forest for logging, and the country was beautiful. The camels, "noble brutes" in Beale's words, were excellent pack animals, exceeding all expectations. He retraced his steps in January and February of 1858 to prove that the road could be used in the winter, and traveled the road twice more in 1859, each time improving the route. At the end of 1859, the Beale Wagon Road was ready for one and all to use—and thousands did, coming across Arizona to reach the West Coast.

Among the travelers moving to the West were sheep ranchers who brought tremendous flocks from New Mexico to California. Once at their destination, they established ranches in the Golden State and were doing well until a devastating drought hit them in the early 1870s. They remembered the spacious green country they had seen around the San Francisco Peaks on their travels, and a handful of them decided to leave their drought-stricken ranches and try their luck in Arizona.

Walking their animals before them, these ranchers traveled the Beale Road back into Arizona, looking for places to relocate. The grasslands around the San Francisco Peaks seemed suitable for sheep ranching, and several of the men settled around the mountains, each one helping himself to grasslands and water where he found them. The ranchers were entering unsurveyed public land subject to no prior claims, and were able to set up ranches wherever they chose under the well-established "first come, first served" code of the West. Those settling around the Peaks were Thomas McMillan, John Clark, Frank Hart, and Charles O'Neill. McMillan was possibly the earliest settler and had established his holdings by May 1876. The land he claimed ran from Antelope Spring northward along Antelope Valley, following the present-day course of the Rio de Flag from the City Dam to the Museum of Northern Arizona. These first settlers proved that Flagstaff was a good place to live, and soon others appeared on the horizon. ❂

This 1876 government map was prepared long before the founding of Flagstaff (represented by the green dot). The trails shown were created by some of the region's earliest pioneers.

Naming the Peaks

HE PEAKS OF SAN FRANCISCO MOUNTAIN, more lovingly know as "the Peaks," are composed of six summits: Doyle, Fremont, Agassiz, Humphreys, Aubineau, and Rees, the first four being the most widely recognized.

HUMPHREYS PEAK, the tallest point in Arizona at 12,633 feet, was named for Brigadier General Andrew Atkinson Humphreys. He was the Chief of the Army Corps of Topographical Engineers and was in charge of the survey data developed by Beale and other early explorers of northern Arizona. Humphreys had a distinguished career as a Union officer in the Civil War, but he was never actually in Arizona.

AGASSIZ PEAK, the next tallest at 12,356 feet, was named for Swiss-born Jean Louis Rodolphe Agassiz, one of the leading naturalists of the Nineteenth Century, who became famous for discovering the Ice Age. As a professor of natural history at Harvard from 1847 to 1873, he enjoyed a worldwide reputation as a scientist. General William Jackson Palmer, who led a railroad surveying expedition through northern Arizona in 1867-68, named the peak in his honor. Even though Agassiz became a Naturalized American, he never made it to Arizona.

FREMONT PEAK, at an elevation of 11,969 feet, was named for John Charles Fremont, famed as The Pathfinder. He mapped the Oregon Trail and was a hero of the Mexican War and the Civil War. He conducted many Western explorations and was the territorial Governor of Arizona from 1878 to 1883. But like Humphreys, Fremont never saw Flagstaff or the Peak named in his honor.

AUBINEAU PEAK, at 11,838 feet, was named for Julius Aubineau, who is regarded as the father of the Flagstaff water system. As Mayor of Flagstaff, he had the power to see the water project through to completion, and in 1898 after miles of pipeline had been laid, Flagstaff experienced its first reliable source of water.

REES PEAK, at an elevation of 11,474, was named after Tom Rees, a local sheep rancher. He served as Clerk of the Board of Supervisors and as Clerk of the Superior Court of Coconino County. He was also active in the Masons and the Elks. Rees Hall at the Federated Church was also named in his honor.

DOYLE PEAK, at 11,460 feet, was also named for a Flagstaff resident. Allen Doyle, born in Detroit, came West in his youth. In 1869, he worked on the construction of the Union Pacific Railroad, being present at the driving of the golden spike. He came to Flagstaff in 1881 as one of the original pioneers and stayed until his death in 1921. He started his life in Flagstaff as a cattle rancher, but had many interests. In 1892, Doyle built a horse trail to the top of the Peaks, and in 1900, he built the first automobile road from Flagstaff to the Grand Canyon. He was frequently employed as a guide and led Zane Grey on several trips. Grey was so impressed with Doyle as being a true man of the West that he fictionalized him in several of his books.

AGASSIZ HUMPHREYS FREMONT AUBINEAU REES DOYLE

ABOVE: *This unique aerial view shows all of the Peaks, including Rees and Aubineau, which are not visible from downtown Flagstaff. (Location of the six peaks provided by USGS)*

Controversy on the Peaks—Selecting place names can be difficult, and there have been quite a few controversies concerning the names on the Peaks. Doyle Saddle, for instance, was originally located between Fremont Peak and Doyle Peak, but today, it is shown as being between Fremont and Agassiz Peaks. Spelling of names has also been a problem. In 1890, the Federal Government created the U.S. Board of Geographic Names in order to resolve such issues. Only the names approved by this board are considered official for Federal maps. The board publishes the approved names in the National Gazetteer of the United States of America, which is the primary authority for checking on the accuracy of names. Today, this work is digitized under the Geographic Names Information System, or GNIS.

A search of GNIS for names of land features on and around the Peaks shows disturbing inconsistencies. For instance,

Aubineau Peak is correctly spelled in GNIS, as is Aubineau Canyon, but the USGS topo maps do not show Aubineau Peak. The topo map shows the canyon spelled "Abineau" on the Humphreys Peak map, but "Aubineau" on the White Horse Hills map. The Forest Service recreation map uses the "Abineau" spelling. The information is even more inconsistent with names honoring Tom Rees. GNIS records it correctly for Rees Peak, but lists it incorrectly for Reese Canyon and Reese Tanks. The topo maps and the Forest Service map display the same error with the canyon and the tanks, but they do not even list Rees Peak.

In the effort of preserving historical accuracy, we deemed it best to reveal this information so that future generations might understand the discrepancies and possibly work to correct them.

THE ARIZONA COLONIZATION COMPANY

OPPOSITE: *This shot was taken in May 1892 by noted photographer William Henry Jackson while he rode the stagecoach from Flagstaff to the Grand Canyon. It perfectly captures the scene the first settlers saw on their arrival in 1876.*

I N 1876, SHORTLY AFTER THE CALIFORNIA sheep ranchers were returning to the lush green of the San Francisco Peaks, two other groups were marching toward the Peaks from the East. They were bands of fifty young men who had been recruited by the Arizona Colonization Company in Boston. The men had paid the company for the right to be guided to northern Arizona where they would establish a farming community on the banks of the Little Colorado River, where in addition to fertile farmland, they were told that they would find a countryside bursting with gold and silver.

The first Boston Party left its home in February 1876, traveled by train to La Junta, Colorado, where they debarked, purchased a few wagons and horses to carry their supplies, and then walked the rest of the way. They arrived at Leroux Spring at the head of Fort Valley on May 1, 1876, and created a farming community. They divided the land into lots, set up a government, and sowed the alpine meadows with grain. When late frosts killed their crops and forays into the mountains showed that they contained no gold or silver, the men decided to fold up their tents at the end of May.

The Second Boston Party, not knowing the fate of the first, left Boston on May 1 and arrived at the farming community about the first of July, expecting to find a thriving village. Instead, there was only a ghost town. Shaken, they decided to disband. Many of the men decided to go to Prescott and turned south. They reached a camping spot in a grassy meadow near Antelope Spring on the Third of July, and found that it was claimed by Thomas McMillan, who graciously gave them permission to camp there.

On the morning of the Fourth of July, 1876, the men of the Second Boston Party had a little Independence Day celebration, using a pine tree as a flag pole. When they moved on, they took their flag with them but left the flag staff, which became a landmark by which the area is known. The City of Flagstaff has constructed a monument at the site on Thorpe Road near the intersection of Navajo Drive. ❁

The Christening

✺

ON THE MORNING OF JULY 4, 1876, the men of the Second Boston Party, who passed through Flagstaff on their way to colonize other parts of the Southwest, celebrated the Centennial—100 years after the signing of the Declaration of Independence. The pine tree they used as a flag pole was left behind when the party moved on, and it eventually led to the name by which Flagstaff is presently known.

The actual name did not stick until years later, when in 1880, the region was rife with railroad construction and crew. The County Seat was located in Prescott, a distant 100 miles away, and even though the county supervisors did not pay much attention to this rowdy little construction camp, they did give the district the generic name of Flag Staff (two words).

Finally, by 1881, Flag Staff had become a sprawling little camp with enough people to qualify for a post office. An official name had to be picked. After numerous proposals were on the table, including Antelope City and Flagpole, Flagstaff was chosen by the citizens, and the name, now spelled as one word, became official. ✺

This 1883 photo shows Old Town, Flagstaff's original business district. Unfortunately, its life was short lived, beginning in April 1880 with the establishment of a construction camp and ending in July 1884 with a fire. The following businesses were located in Old Town: twelve saloons, a dance hall, five stores, five cafés, one hotel, a brewery, a cobbler shop, a livery, and two hand laundries.

ABOVE: *This is the first photo of New Town, taken in the fall of 1883. The building on the right was the P. B. Brannen General Store, a fine stone building costing $10,000, a small fortune in those days. The wooden building was James Vail's saloon. The street in front of the buildings is Railroad Avenue (now Route 66), and the street between them is present-day San Francisco Street.*

OPPOSITE: *Flagstaff owes its existence to the railroad, and it seems that these women felt right at home on one of the big locomotives that brought prosperity to the town. Their clothing dates the time of the photo to 1912.*

THE RAILROAD

✦

IN ORDER TO AID IN THE SETTLEMENT OF the West, Congress offered lucrative incentives to railroad companies to build lines across the western lands. In 1866, a charter to build the Atlantic & Pacific Railroad (A&P) across northern Arizona was granted, but the railroad company had trouble raising money. By fits and starts it finally pushed a line from Kansas to Albuquerque, by which time the charter rights had been sold to the Atchison, Topeka, and Santa Fe Railroad. With this benefactor providing new funds, the A&P was finally ready to make the final push from Albuquerque to California in 1880.

In April 1880, Lewis Kingman, leading a party of surveyors, established a little construction camp in northern Arizona where they found a spring near present-day Flagstaff. For several months afterwards, various contractors moved in and out of the camp, grading, tie-chopping, and performing other preliminary tasks in order to prepare the line for the rails, which were laid by special large crews called The Front.

During the months that the railroad construction flourished, there were hundreds of crew-members at work around the Flagstaff area. The workers were mainly young men looking for constant entertainment. Almost overnight the construction camp began to sprout enterprises designed to separate the workmen from their wages. Many were legitimate businesses such as cafés and hotels, but even more numerous and popular were the saloons, gambling halls, and brothels. A visitor once counted twenty-one thriving saloons in the camp even though a bottle of beer cost a wallet-straining dollar.

Because this region was located in Yavapai County with the county seat—and the law—in Prescott, a man's own six-gun became the preferred method for settling disputes. This kept up throughout the period of construction. At one point, Flagstaff was even labeled as "the wildest town in Arizona," as shootings, stabbings, and even dynamitings were all too frequent.

The actual railroad reached the eastern edge of Canyon Diablo, some thirty miles east of Flagstaff, on December 19, 1881 and paused there while a bridge was built. The crew, comprised of several hundred men, was held up at the Canyon for seven months waiting for the bridge to be finished, and many found Flagstaff an alluring place to spend their time. On July 1, 1882, the bridge was ready and the crews continued laying track toward Flagstaff.

When the rails reached Flagstaff in August, they continued westward, hardly breaking stride, and the construction boom ended. The Front, which had made up most of Flagstaff's first citizens, followed the rails westward. But hardly had the train gone out of sight than a new whistle was heard, the shrill blast from E. E. Ayer's lumber mill, which first sounded on August 19, 1882. Many of the men who had come to work on the railroad decided to stay on and work at the mill, which firmly cemented Flagstaff as a permanent community. ✦

NEW SANTA FE DEPOT, FLAGSTAFF, ARIZONA.

110573

LEFT: *This photo proudly displays the 1927 Flagstaff Depot, which is still in use today.*
BOTTOM: *This modern shot of the depot shows that it has changed very little since 1927.*

OPPOSITE TOP: *This is the front of the depot that served Flagstaff from 1889-1927. The men are probably traveling salesmen, who rode the line from town to town. Situated near the current depot, this historic building was renovated in 1999 and is being used for the offices of the BNSF Railroad.*
OPPOSITE BOTTOM: *The boxcars shown in the left foreground with steps leading up to their doors made up the first Flagstaff depot. At first, the depot consisted of one boxcar. Then the town grew and a second car was added. By the time Flagstaff had grown to a four-car depot, the town leaders protested so strongly that the railroad built a real depot in 1888. Shortly after it was built, however, it burned, and the stone building shown above was built to replace it in 1889.*

THE LUMBER INDUSTRY

❋

IF IT WASN'T FOR E. E. AYER, THE CHICAGO
Industrialist, Flagstaff might not have seen
much of a future. As the railroad construction
crews were moving out and Flagstaff's population was
dwindling, Ayer took advantage of the nation's largest
ponderosa forest surrounding the town. On August 19,
1882, he opened the Ayer Lumber Company with a steady
payroll for hundreds of workers, both in the woods and
at the mill.

Ayer was a family man, so he started a company town
around the mill in order to better support his employees
and their families. In 1884, he hired D. M. (Matt) Riordan
as manager, selling the mill outright to him in 1887.
Matt brought in his half-brothers, T. A. (Tim) and M. J.
(Mike) Riordan. The Riordans, like Ayer, were calm family
men, and together, they did much to bring culture and
refinement to Flagstaff.

By 1910, Flagstaff had the reputation of being a lumber
town with three big lumber mills in full operation: the
Arizona Lumber and Timber Company, the Greenlaw
Lumber Mill, and the new Flagstaff Lumber Manufacturing
Company. The mills enjoyed solid growth, and then a
boom during World War I. But a sharp unforeseen postwar depression shook the industry and caused a major
shift in the operation of the mills. The Arizona Lumber
and Timber Company cut back production to low levels,
the Greenlaw Lumber Mill was closed permanently, and
the Flagstaff Lumber Manufacturing Company went
bankrupt. The depression also affected the separate
community of Milton, located around the Arizona
Lumber and Timber Company. In 1920, the small family-
oriented town was annexed by Flagstaff. The only
reminder of the company town around the mill was
the name of Milton Road.

The remnants of the Flagstaff Lumber Manufacturing
Company were purchased in 1925 and incorporated
into the Cady Lumber Company, which began large-scale
operations in Flagstaff and McNary. In 1931, the grip of
the national depression began to tighten around Flagstaff's
throat and the Cady Lumber Mill closed, throwing
scores of men out of work. The Arizona Lumber and

BOTTOM: *Flagstaff's lumber companies built
logging railroads to bring timber to the mills. This
photo demonstrates the huge size and fine quality
of the Ponderosa pines in the first-growth forests
around Flagstaff. The last logging train in
Flagstaff blew its whistle in 1966, as trucks took
over all log hauling.*

OPPOSITE: *These workers at the Arizona Lumber
and Timber Company demonstrate the kind of
manpower that was needed to do millwork. The
mill shown here burned down in 1898 and was
rebuilt only to burn down again in 1961.*

Timber Company, which had revived during the twenties, was also hit by the Great Depression. First it slowed down, trying to keep a payroll going for the benefit of the workers, but eventually it suspended all operations.

The Riordan era in the Flagstaff lumber industry ended in 1933 when Tim Riordan sold out to Joe Dolan. Dolan reopened the Arizona Lumber and Timber Company to half capacity. By 1935, economic conditions were so much improved that Joe Dolan began running the sawmill full-time, giving jobs to over four hundred workers.

The year 1937 saw the former Cady Lumber Company come out of bankruptcy under new ownership and a new name, Southwest Lumber Mills. The saws began turning again and hundreds more Flagstaff men went back to work. A few years later, in 1940, the Arizona Lumber and Timber Company also saw a change of hands as Joe Dolan sold out to the Saginaw-Manistee Lumber Company.

Another major player in the lumber business was added in 1950 when the Kaibab Lumber Company began operating in Flagstaff. It was formed after the owners bought and consolidated the smaller Babbitt's Lumber Mill and the Oak Creek Lumber Company. This meant that, once again, Flagstaff had three big mills operating full time: Southwest Lumber Mills, Saginaw-Manistee Lumber Company, and Kaibab Lumber Company.

In 1953, a new owner who realized the potential of the building boom bought the Southwest Lumber Mill and began to turn the company into a giant. He purchased the Saginaw-Manistee Lumber Company in 1953, consolidated the operations into one company, and in 1954, shut down the old mill. Hundreds had worked there over the years and looked on the closure as the loss of an old friend. This reduced the town's lumber mills from three to two, but Southwest, which soon changed

TOP LEFT: *The prize lumberjacks, recruited from the northwoods of Michigan, Wisconsin, and Minnesota, were the Swedes. This hardy group, depicted in front of the mess hall (their favorite place) was known as the Musical Logging Swedes.*
TOP RIGHT: *When the big trees were felled and trimmed, they were cut into sections and dragged to the logging railroad by these big wheels pulled by huge draft horses. Tractors and other motor-driven equipment replaced the horses in the 1920s.*

RIGHT: *There were no chain saws for the early-day lumberjacks. They worked in expert two-man teams, first chopping a notch to control the fall of the tree, as shown here. Then they would drop the tree with a handsaw, each man vigorously pulling one end. Tall stumps, still seen in the Flagstaff woods today, are evidence of this historic hand-cutting method.* BOTTOM: *The Greenlaw Lumber Mill, shown here, operated on the east side of town where the Flagstaff Mall is currently located. It was a large, successful operation for many years, but had to close its doors in 1920. No vestiges of it remain today.*

its name to Southwest Forest Industries, grew so large that its workforce increased to some five hundred men, replacing all of the jobs that had been lost through consolidation of the mills. Finally, in the 1970s, Southwest also bought and absorbed the Kaibab Lumber Company, reducing the industry to one giant mill.

An overlooked problem that had been simmering for decades finally doomed the Flagstaff lumber industry. Scientists had vastly overrated the ability of the forest to regenerate. It was clear by the 1980s that pine trees were not growing fast enough to replace the trees that had been cut, and therefore, there were not enough big trees left to harvest. In 1993, Flagstaff's last surviving mill, Southwest Forest Industries, finally closed its doors. This act marked the end of large-scale logging in Flagstaff. ✵

THE RIORDANS

T HE FIRST OF THE RIORDANS TO COME TO Flagstaff was Denis Matthew Riordan (1848-1928), who arrived in 1884, making him one of the town's earliest pioneers. He had been working as an Indian agent for the federal government and had caught the eye of E. E. Ayer, the owner of Flagstaff's first lumber mill, the Ayer Lumber Company. Ayer offered the job of General Manager to Matt, who saw that there would be great opportunity in the enterprise, and accepted the offer.

In 1886, Matt brought his half-brother Timothy Allen Riordan (1858-1946) into the business as Superintendent. Matt bought the mill from Ayer in 1887, renaming it the Arizona Lumber Company. It was at this time that Matt added another half-brother, Michael James Riordan (1865–1930) to the staff. The trio managed the mill successfully for several years until 1893 when they had a disagreement about the operation of the mill, causing Matt to withdraw from the business. He left Flagstaff in 1897. Tim and Mike bought Matt's interests and incorporated the business, naming it the Arizona Lumber and Timber Company. Around the same time, Tim and Mike married sisters from Cincinnati, Caroline and Elizabeth Metz.

The company was the area's largest employer for many years, with up to three hundred men on the payroll, and it eventually became the largest lumber mill in the Southwest. The Riordans built a company town around the mill, called Milltown, which Mike later changed to Milton in order to honor the English poet. The brothers became the unofficial mayors of Milton, and they operated it in a paternal fashion that always kept the best interest of their workers in mind.

The Riordans came to Flagstaff to stay and believed in giving something back to their town. Well-educated, cultured, and progressive, they supported every endeavor to improve Flagstaff and its quality of life. Only Mike ever became an elected public official, but they were so well known, respected, and influential that they had many political and civic achievements to their credit. They played an essential role in the creation of Coconino County and the construction of its courthouse, the construction of the Reform School building and its later metamorphosis into Northern Arizona Normal School, and the achievement of statehood for Arizona. They built Lake Mary and allowed the public to use it. They were also instrumental in placing Flagstaff on the National Old Trails Highway, which later became Route 66. In all, the Riordans were honest, hard working, and intelligent, and they helped set a high standard of living for Flagstaff and its future generations. ❋

BELOW: *T. A. Riordan was such an important figure in the drive for Arizona and New Mexico statehood, that he was invited to attend the signing of both statehood bills. Here he stands in the upper left-hand corner on the White House steps with the New Mexico contingent on January 6, 1912.*

OPPOSITE: *The Riordan brothers, Tim and Mike, built adjoining homes connected by a shared recreation room. Famed architect Charles Whittlesey, who later designed the El Tovar Hotel at the Grand Canyon, drew the plans. Work started in 1903 and was finished in 1904. At that time, the homes sat by themselves out in the country, but since then, numerous businesses, homes, and the university have grown up around the property. The Riordan family eventually donated the homes to the State of Arizona, which created the Riordan Mansion State Historic Park.*

THE LIVESTOCK INDUSTRIES

❈

SHEEP

T HE FIRST ANGLO SETTLERS TO THE Flagstaff region were the sheep ranchers who arrived in 1876. They could claim free range rights on unsurveyed government land wherever they chose, and federal tariffs guaranteed high prices. Sheep thrived in Flagstaff's summer climate, and ranchers avoided the harsh winters by walking the animals to the desert. When the railroad arrived in 1882, it attracted cattle ranchers and farmers to the area, but sheep and cattlemen quickly learned to live side-by-side and Flagstaff never had any range wars.

Northern Arizona, with Flagstaff in the lead, became one of the prime sheep ranching centers in America, with about 700,000 animals scouring the rangelands in 1890. During that decade, however, the free and easy days of ranching began to tighten up. The government surveyed the land and built fences, the Forest Service took over range management, and lastly, anti-sheep sentiment in Washington DC led to a threatening ban on grazing in the federal forests. Through all of these threats, Flagstaff ranchers still stayed strong well into the 20th century, and even remained Flagstaff's number one industry. But by the Second World War, synthetic fabrics like nylon began to cut the demand for wool. After the war, the industry suffered a steady shrinkage, and today, there are only four families raising about 20,000 sheep.

ABOVE: *Open grassy valleys were favorite places to graze sheep. In this shot, hundreds of them contentedly chew the grass on the floor of a mountain meadow while their owner watches. Note the man and children in the carriage—possibly members of the rancher's family come to pay a visit.*

LEFT: *Sheep were often dipped in creosote to kill any vermin that lived in their wool. It was a messy, unpleasant, but necessary process. Notice that the men are wet from the creosote that was shaken off by the sheep after they emerged from their dunking.*

CATTLE

The land around Flagstaff has always been good cattle country, and as soon as the arrival of the railroad made cattle ranching feasible, the ranchers quickly moved in. The railroad was able to offer federal grant land for sale at fifty cents an acre, and the Atlantic and Pacific Railroad sold one million acres to the "Hashknife Outfit" east of Flagstaff and 250,000 acres to the "A-1 Company" north of town. At first, the ranchers who bought railroad acreage had trouble because when the acreage was surveyed, they found sheep ranchers, homesteaders, and other squatters already settled on the land. A period of unrest followed while claims were disputed and boundaries were established. Once their rights were in place, business did not get easier for many ranchers as they learned that the giant outfits were hard to run and manage. Drought, blizzards, and rustling caused major losses.

Finally, the Great Depression of the 1930s forced many marginal ranchers out of business. By mid-century, ranching was not a game for the small operator with a head full of Western dreams. Sound range management skills and marketing expertise were necessary. Today, even though the number of ranches and animals is shrinking, cattle ranching is still a viable industry and honest-to-goodness cowboys still walk the streets of Flagstaff. ❈

ABOVE: *Cattle graze peacefully at the CO Bar's summer ranch in the high country. The San Francisco Peaks tower majestically in the background.* BELOW: *Calf branding was tough work, and it took many hands to get the job done, especially since the calves did not like being branded. In most cases, the cowboys had to throw the calves to the ground, which required a lot of strength and patience.*

THE THREE FIRES

✻

FLAGSTAFF AS A RAILROAD CAMP HAD been a rough-looking place. Because no one knew whether the town would remain after the construction boom had passed by, many of the structures were temporary, built of logs or canvas, and could readily be sacrificed by their owners if they chose to move.

Railroad officials did not plan to have a town at Flagstaff, either. But since they had to stop somewhere to get water for their steam engines and there was already a small community in place, they decided to take advantage of the situation and set up a depot. They did not like the site of the existing town for their depot, however, because it was on a slope on the south edge of Mars Hill. So in the fall of 1882, they relocated the depot about one mile east, where they owned some flat land south of present day Route 66 just east of San Francisco Street. The depot was only a boxcar, and through the winter of 1882-1883, it sat by itself on that location. The railroad's engineering department was then instructed to map out a town site on the land that it owned just north of the new depot. This was done early in 1883, and the company offered lots for sale at twenty-five dollars each, or even cheaper by the dozen. While this was going on, the merchants of Flagstaff who were located in Old Town watched goods being loaded and unloaded at the depot and people getting on and off the train in the New Town district. By the summer of 1883, it seemed to some of them that they should relocate closer to the action, so they bought lots and began to build.

P. J. Brannen, a merchant who had started out at the railroad camp in a tent selling general merchandise, was the first to move his business to the new town. He went all out and invested his money in a grand stone building just across the road from the depot on the northeast corner of Route 66 and San Francisco Street. Soon to follow was Jim Vail, who put up a saloon just across the street on the northwest corner of that intersection.

Their efforts were rewarded with success, and soon there was a land rush to the new business district, with storefronts going up all along the street fronting the depot. By the summer of 1884 there were two Flagstaffs, commonly called Old Town and New Town.

Unfortunately for Old Town, a fire started later that year when a dancehall girl kicked over a lantern, destroying everything it could reach, including homes. The homes were rebuilt, but the area was finished as a business location. Thereafter all commercial construction was in New Town, and soon that label disappeared—now there was only Flagstaff.

Aside from Brannen's stone building, all of Flagstaff's buildings were made of wood from the lumber mill, and soon there was a solid string of buildings, most of which were saloons, along Railroad Avenue (present-day Route 66). On Valentine's Day 1886, New Town's first terrible fire raged through the district, destroying thirty buildings in thirty minutes.

Some people thought that the fire was the end of Flagstaff, but the town rebounded and even survived a second devastating fire in 1888. Afterwards, every property owner who could afford the price rebuilt out of fire-resistant masonry or brick. After the 1888 fire, Front Street began to acquire the solid look that still stands today. ✻

After multiple fires devastated the downtown business section in the 1880s, the property owners began to rebuild using bricks and stone to make their buildings more fire resistant. This was spurred by a city ordinance passed in 1896, which designated the main section of downtown as a fire district within which no wooden buildings were allowed. The results are seen in this 1917 photo, where only one wooden building remains.

THE BABBITTS

THERE WERE FIVE BABBITT BROTHERS, David (1858-1929), George (1860-1920), William (1863-1930), Charles (1865-1956), and Edward (1868-1943). They were born in Cincinnati, Ohio, the sons of a prosperous grocer. The boys were well educated, with the expectation that they would all work in the grocery business with the exception of Edward, who took a law degree.

In spite of the comfortable berth that was assured them at home, the older boys became enamored of the West and wanted to seek their fortunes in the cattle business. Starting in 1884 they began taking time off to scout likely locations where they could buy land and cattle and start a new life as ranchers. On April 7, 1886, David and William checked out the brand-new town of Flagstaff—or what was left of it after the Valentine's Day Fire of 1886. The town was rebuilding from the ashes, but it still appealed to the brothers. Investing their stake of $20,000, they bought ranch land and a starter herd of cattle on behalf of the family. Using the soon-to-become famous CO Bar brand on their cattle, which stood for Cincinnati, Ohio, they began carving out a solid future.

Charles joined David and William in the summer of 1886. George wound up the brothers' Ohio business and came to Flagstaff in 1887. Edward was the latecomer, coming to Flagstaff only after he finished his law degree in 1891. In spite of a promising start, being elected Probate Judge for Coconino County in 1892 and a member of the Arizona legislature in 1894, Edward chose to leave Flagstaff and returned to Cincinnati in 1896.

A neighbor of the Babbitt family in Cincinnati was Gerhard Verkamp, a well-to-do merchant who had several daughters. Three of the Babbitt brothers married three of the Verkamp sisters: David married Emma, Charles married Mary, and Edward married Matilda. Papa Verkamp thought highly of his new sons and stood ready to give them advice and financial support. With this help, the four brothers who stayed in Flagstaff proceeded to carve out a business empire.

They had barely gotten their feet wet in the cattle business before a fickle market showed them that it was a tough way to make a living. Papa Verkamp advised them to diversify, and they followed his advice with gusto. From cattle ranching they branched out into retail merchandising and sheep ranching. They went into the trading post business and built a string of two-dozen posts across the reservation. And over the years, they owned a mortuary, an ice plant, an auto dealership, a bank, a slaughterhouse, a meat packing plant, a fox farm, and a host of other businesses.

In building their business empire, they did not neglect their civic duties. David Babbitt was the town's first acting mayor. George was Coconino County Treasurer, and Edward was Probate Judge. They were active in the creation of Coconino County, the incorporation of Flagstaff, and the creation of Northern Arizona Normal School, which later became Northern Arizona University.

OPPOSITE: *This 1908 shot shows a scene on Aspen Avenue in front of Babbitts' Department Store. A sheepherder has loaded his burros with provisions for an extended stay in the forest. The woman in the white dress crossing the unpaved street has hiked up her skirt to keep the hem from dragging in the dirt that fills the street.*

RIGHT: *The five Babbitt brothers, all from Cincinnati, pose for a group portrait. From left to right they are Edward, Charles, David, George, and William. All of them permanently moved to Flagstaff except for Edward, who returned to Cincinnati after a few years.*

They were also builders who left their stamp on the Flagstaff landscape, especially downtown where several of the buildings they constructed are still in use.

Except for Edward, the other four Babbitt brothers spent the rest of their lives in Flagstaff, raising families, attending to business, and improving the town. Many young men came west in the 1800s to seek their fortunes. Of those few who succeeded, many took their money back home to spend it in style. A very few stayed, made fortunes, and used their money to improve their adopted towns. The Babbitts were among these select few and did much to make Flagstaff the successful town it is today. ❖

OPPOSITE: *This is the original Babbitt store, built in 1888, with some of the brothers, family, and employees standing at the entrance. Aspen Avenue, with the town's first church in view, is to the left. San Francisco Street is to the right.*

RIGHT: *This is the building in 1897 showing the 1891 expansion. There are now eight windows in the upper story on the San Francisco Street side.*
TOP LEFT: *This is the fully developed Babbitt Department Store in the late 1940s, showing all of the additions to the original building with sixteen windows in the upper story on the San Francisco Street side.* TOP MIDDLE: *This is the store after it was modernized in 1957 with a streamlined white facing.* TOP RIGHT: *This photo shows today's version of the building. In 1990, approximately half of the building on the Aspen Avenue side was cut away and the 1957 facing was removed, restoring the old, classic look of the building.*

This 1907 photo depicts the rough work of the cowboys performing the annual spring ritual of branding newborn calves. William Babbitt, the brother who ran the ranches, is in the center of the background with his hands on his hips.

This is a modern shot of cowboys on the Babbitt ranch, the CO Bar, and it shows that not much has changed when it comes to branding.

EARLY FLAGSTAFF BUSINESSES

THE EARLIEST FLAGSTAFF BUSINESSES were those established in Old Town beginning in 1880. Among these pioneer enterprises were seven saloons, three restaurants, two general stores, two laundries, a newsstand, a boot shop, a livery, a hotel, and a brewery. One of the hardest tasks faced by the operators was to get supplies, most of which were laboriously brought in by wagon from Prescott. Once the railroad reached town in 1882, supplies flowed in swiftly, and it was possible to stock the latest goods from Los Angeles to Chicago.

As the business district shifted from Old Town to New Town—a move that was completed by 1884—a strip of buildings developed along Railroad Avenue, which is present-day Route 66. At first, saloons dominated the scene. But before long, business owners recognized that there were more practical needs not being met and responded by opening up shops of every kind. Flagstaff farmers supplied locally-grown vegetables and grains, and the area's large ranching industry made beef and lamb plentiful.

All of the pioneer businesses were locally owned and operated. The majority of the new businesses were small, but there was one giant—Babbitt Brothers, whose sprawling department store grew to be the largest in the Arizona territory. There was some external competition from mail order firms such as Sears, Roebuck & Co., but not enough to hurt the local stores. The first chain store, J. C. Penney, did not appear in Flagstaff until 1917, and due to the continuing growth of the town, local merchants easily withstood its competition and continued to prosper. In fact, most of them considered the appearance of the store as a welcome sign that Flagstaff was progressing.

The Southside developed a few businesses of its own, and when Route 66 came through town in 1926, some roadside establishments were extended along its path. There were several neighborhood markets, and distinct Southside and East Flagstaff business areas. However, all of the major stores were located in the historic downtown district and it was the place where Flagstaff residents came to buy a pair of shoes, have a tooth pulled, do their banking, see a movie, or have a meal in a café. It was classic small town America—the residents knew the business people and the business people knew their customers.

Over the years, the Downtown business district did see its share of hard times. But in the late 1990s, local care and restoration brought it back to its friendly small town roots with most businesses being locally owned and operated. Once again, you can walk up San Francisco Street and see smiling faces and local Flagstaff charm. ❖

A customer rests against a counter in the grocery department at Babbitts', circa 1900. Fine groceries of every kind were neatly stacked, and at that time, there was no self-service. Clerks who really knew the business helped customers.

These women, very nicely dressed, shop for fabric in Babbitts' dry goods department in the late 1890s. Waiting on them from behind the counter from right to left are John Verkamp, David Babbitt, and an unknown man.

TOP: *This shot shows the original Brannen store building, the first building in downtown Flagstaff. This is how it looked circa 1914 when it was the New York Store, owned and operated by K. J. Nackard. The New York Store was popular at the time due to its fashionable merchandise and upscale wares.* RIGHT: *This is the interior of Black's Bar taken around 1907. This saloon, one of the most popular in Flagstaff, was located at the NW corner of San Francisco Street and Railroad Avenue (present-day Route 66).* BOTTOM: *This is the interior of the wooden building shown on page 23, which was used for many years as a news stand, as it was in 1910 when this photo was taken. The proprietor sold tobacco products as well as popular periodicals.*

OPPOSITE: *In addition to the many saloons that quenched the thirst of Flagstaff citizens, there were also local breweries. In this shot, Pete Berry, owner of the San Juan Saloon at 6 E. Route 66 had just received a shipment of beer and the locals were lined up and ready to test the new batch. Berry eventually left Flagstaff to pursue mining interests at the Grand Canyon, built the first hotel at the South Rim, the Grandview, and became a pioneer of Grand Canyon tourism.*

ABOVE: *This building's first life was that of a harness shop.* LEFT: *The harness shop took on a new form when it was remodeled with a fancy river pebble finish and opened as the Power Hat Shop.* BELOW: *The building is still used today. It is located at 113 E. Aspen Avenue.*

BOTTOM: *The building at 9 North Leroux Street was built in 1911 by Dr. R. O. Raymond as a combination medical office and residence.* TOP: *This modern-day photo is proof of the value of the sturdy brick construction used during the early 1900s. As the photo displays, few changes have been made to the exterior.*

JOHN WEATHERFORD
AND THE HOTEL

JOHN W. WEATHERFORD, AN EARLY FLAGSTAFF pioneer, was born in 1859 in Texas, leaving home as a teenager to explore the mining towns of the West. He was passing through Flagstaff in 1886 on his way to a copper boom in Montana, but after taking one look at the San Francisco Peaks, he fell in love. He stayed in Flagstaff for the rest of his life. After trying several businesses—a saloon, a stage line, a livery stable—he found his calling as a merchant of men's clothing.

In 1898, he erected a two-story sandstone building on a lot on the southwest corner of Aspen Avenue and Leroux Street. He located his Gents' Furnishings store in the bottom half and lived upstairs with his wife, Margaret, and son, Hugh. A year later, he began construction on an adjoining two-story building, resulting in the creation of the Weatherford Hotel.

The hotel opened on January 1, 1900, and was a big success. For years it was regarded as Flagstaff's finest. Zane Grey had a suite on the second floor where, according to local legend, he wrote parts of "The Call of the Canyon."

In 1929, the beautiful woodwork balcony that adorned the building was badly damaged by fire and had to be removed. Five years later, Weatherford died. Fortunately for Flagstaff, the hotel lived on. The present owners bought the building in 1974 and began a comprehensive program of restoration, bringing the hotel back to prime condition by 1998. Today, the historic Weatherford Hotel is a beloved downtown landmark.

The Fourth of July has always been a big day in Flagstaff. The town got its namesake on July 4, 1876, when the Second Boston Party raised a flag staff, so Flagstaff citizens have always had an extra reason to celebrate the event. On July 4, 1908, the Babbitt Brothers entered this elaborate float in a parade held that year. One of the Babbitt enterprises was a meat-packing plant where they made sausages. The girl in the float was the sausage queen and is decked with garlands of sausage. The sign visible on the south wall of the Weatherford Hotel was painted in January 1900, and the balcony, which was quite impressive for its time, was a favorite place for Flagstaff citizens to view the festive parades.

RIGHT: *John W. Weatherford built the Weatherford Hotel on the corner of Leroux and Aspen, opening it for business on New Year's Day in 1900. Note the balcony wrapping around the building in this photo taken in 1915.*

WEATHERFORD HOTEL, FLAGSTAFF, ARIZONA

ABOVE: *The balcony burned in 1929 and was removed, along with the witch's cap.* BOTTOM: *In 1999, the balcony was partly restored, giving the building its present charming appearance.*

OPPOSITE: *The parade shown here was held on the Fourth of July in 1907. A prize was given for the best dressed cowboy. The Weatherford Hotel stands in the background, displaying its full balcony and original witch's cap.*

HOTEL WEATHERFORD

GATEWAY TO THE GRAND CANYON

FLAGSTAFF'S ECONOMY HAS LONG BEEN based on tourism, and it began as early as 1892 when the Board of Trade entered into an agreement with the railroad to run a stagecoach from Flagstaff to the Grand Canyon. This giant step opened up the natural wonder to the world and put Flagstaff on the map as the Gateway to the Grand Canyon.

The new Grand Canyon Stage Coach Line was a success and stimulated investment and construction in the heart of the city, producing several new business—most notably two hotels. In 1899, John Weatherford started construction of the Weatherford Hotel, which is still located at the northwest corner of Leroux Street and Aspen Avenue, and J. J. "Sandy" Donahue started building the Commercial Hotel, which was sadly destroyed by fire in 1975.

Unfortunately, the Grand Canyon Stage Coach was short-lived. On September 17, 1901, the first train from Williams rolled into the Grand Canyon station, putting an end to Flagstaff's tourism claim on the Canyon. Nearly sixty years had to pass before Grand Canyon travel was again brought back to Flagstaff. With the opening of Highway 180 in 1960, tourists could originate their Grand Canyon trips from Flagstaff instead of Williams or Cameron. Also in 1960, the Black Canyon Highway, which would become I-17, was opened. And even though it was not yet divided all the way, it gave Phoenix visitors a much better and faster connection to Arizona's Natural Wonder.

By 1993, tourism to the Grand Canyon was at an all-time high with five million visitors a year. Planners predicted that this upswing in visitation would continue and began planning for the expected numbers of the coming future. Today, the Grand Canyon is one of the most visited Natural Wonders in the World, and Flagstaff still has the honor of being the gateway.

One of the popular attractions at the Grand Canyon is the Hopi House, which opened in 1905. It has had many famous visitors over the years, including Albert Einstein and his wife, shown here with a Hopi family. Einstein is wearing a very non-Hopi feather headdress.

The favorite route of the Grand Canyon stagecoach took it right up Leroux Street, and from
1892 to 1900, residents along the street had to
accustom themselves in the summer to hearing the
iron wheels of the big coaches crunch the gravel at
seven o'clock in the morning as the line began its
twelve-hour run to the Canyon.

OPPOSITE: *The stagecoach to the Grand Canyon was put out of business by the train that began to run to the South Rim in 1901. In time, the rail-road business would be eclipsed by the popularity of the automobile.*

RIGHT: *This representative view from the South Rim shows what millions come to see each year—the sublime beauty of the Grand Canyon. Through the first few decades of the 1900s, travel to the Grand Canyon was difficult at best. But in 1922, ex-Army pilot Captain R. V. Thomas landed the first plane at Indian Gardens— more of a stunt flight than anything to do with transportation. Within a few years, however, there was regular air travel to the Canyon, making it more accessible than ever before.*

COCONINO COUNTY COURTHOUSE

✳

COCONINO COUNTY, WITH FLAGSTAFF AS its seat, was created in 1891 while Arizona was still a territory. The new county needed a courthouse, but the law required that congress had to sign a bill approving the sale of bonds to finance its construction. There was no such bond bill in 1891, so for the first months of the county's life, officials had to rent office space wherever they could find it, scattering the offices all over town.

The Babbitt family came to the rescue, offering to build an addition to their store if the county would rent the upper story. The deal was made, and as a result, the first Coconino County courthouse was upstairs in the Babbitt Building. This consolidation of offices into one space helped, but the desire to have a proper courthouse stayed firm.

Federal approval for Coconino County courthouse bonds was not obtained until the summer of 1894, when Flagstaff lumber magnate D. M. Riordan went to Washington. His efforts worked and the bill finally passed. Even though the funding was limited to a paltry $15,000, the county went to work immediately and invited architects to submit plans on a competitive bid basis. The winning design was for a two-story red sandstone building topped with a clock tower. Ground was broken in October 1894.

By August 1, 1895, the building was finished and county offices were up and running in the new structure. The Coconino County courthouse was a jewel. It was well-situated and had an air of grandeur. It was not only functional but was a monument to the pioneer spirit and enterprise that had helped create Flagstaff. The only flaw was the empty clock tower, left vacant due to the shortage of funds.

The original building served the county's needs until the 1920s, when population growth forced expansion. In 1925, the county built a matching addition on the east side of the original building. Citizens were pleased to see that the project included the installation of clocks in the tower. As the county continued to grow, more additions were tacked onto the building in the 1950s, '60s, and '70s, until it became such a mix of architectural styles that it detracted from the building's appearance. Much of this mismatched clutter was remedied in the Twenty-first Century when the worst add-on, a cheap 1950s west wing, was removed and the building was restored to its original look, a project that was finished in 2002. Now the stately courthouse presides over downtown once again. ✵

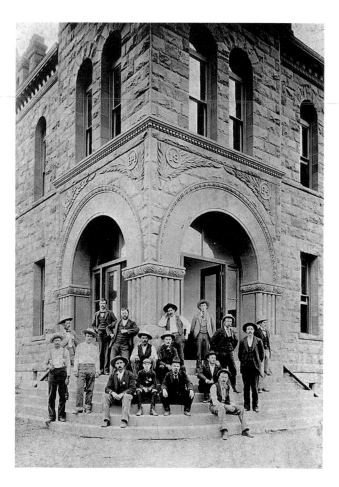

OPPOSITE: *To accommodate population growth, the Coconino County Courthouse has been expanded several times since the original part was built in 1894. This photo shows the 1925 addition. The expansion included the placement of clocks in the south and west faces of the tower.*

RIGHT: *Coconino County was created in 1891, but it was not until 1894 that the county had a courthouse. The county officials gathered around the steps of the new building when this photo was taken in 1895 to celebrate its official opening.*

OPPOSITE: *Here is the original 1894 courthouse, sitting by itself on the edge of town. It was a nice building considering that it was built for $15,000, which was not even enough to buy clocks for the clock tower.*

LEFT: *Another wing was added to the courthouse in 1956, again in 1968, and yet again in 1979, resulting in an unattractive mishmash of styles. County officials undertook construction of new buildings in the 1990s. Just visible at the top left of this photo is the administration building, which houses the Recorder, County Attorney, Treasurer, and Assessor. A bit later, the new courts building in the mid-left of the photo was added. In conjunction with its construction, the original courthouse was renovated, removing the 1956 wing. Shown here is the dedication ceremony in August 2002.*

SPACE EXPLORATION

✤

T HE YEAR 1894 BROUGHT A REMARKABLE prize to Flagstaff citizens, who knew that their town was a contender in the hunt for the location of Lowell Observatory. In April, they beamed with pride at the news that Lowell had chosen Flagstaff as the observatory site. Other possible locations had been Tombstone, Tucson, Tempe, Phoenix, and Prescott, but Flagstaff had the edge due to its good, clean air.

Over the years, Lowell Observatory has been home to many newsworthy events. In 1914, V. M. Slipher, an astronomer at Lowell Observatory, presented a paper at a scientific convention concerning a project he had been working on for years: the red shift and the expanding universe. The group began listening to the presentation with skepticism but finished with rousing applause. The assembled scientists knew they had heard the first word on something of huge significance. Slipher had presented the underpinnings for today's dominant scientific theory about the origin of the universe, the Big Bang.

Lowell built an observatory worthy of grand things, but in November 1916, Percival Lowell, who had done so much for the town, died in his mansion on Mars Hill. He is buried there in a mausoleum that was designed by his widow.

LOWELL LIBRARY   FLAGSTAFF, ARIZONA

RIGHT: *This is Dr. Eugene M. Shoemaker, the world-class scientist who was responsible for moving the USGS facility to Flagstaff in 1963. This photo portrays him in 1964 testing a prototype spacesuit as part of the Apollo Project preparations.*

BELOW: *In order to prepare astronauts for a moon landing, a scale model of the moon landing site was prepared in the black cinder hills north of town. Blasting was necessary to replicate the craters of the moon.*

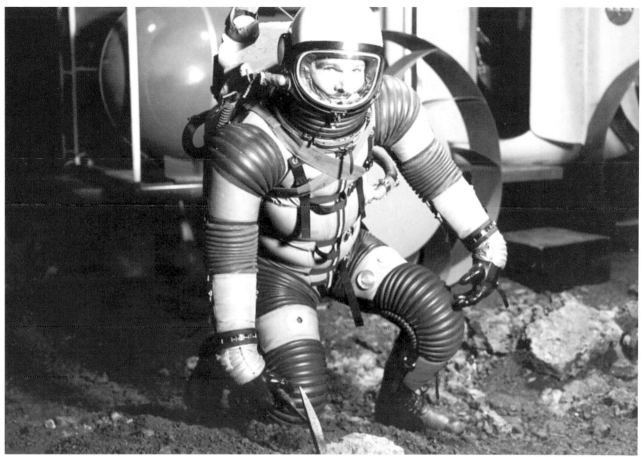

OPPOSITE LEFT: *The administration building at Lowell Observatory, affectionately called The Dome, housed the scientists who worked there. Today, the campus is much larger with many buildings dotting the hilltop.*

OPPOSITE RIGHT: *Percival Lowell began building Lowell Observatory in 1894, establishing Flagstaff in the forefront of scientific communities in the West. Dr. Lowell, who believed there was life on Mars, spent many hours looking for proof of his theories through the lens of his big Clark telescope.*

Fortunately for the scientific community, the Observatory continued in Lowell's wonderful tradition of exploration and discovery, when in 1930, they announced to the world that Flagstaff astronomer Clyde Tombaugh had discovered a new planet. In keeping with the style of mythological names, the planet was lovingly named Pluto because the first two letters of the name, PL, were the initials of Percival Lowell.

Because Flagstaff had established its name in the scientific community, another facility added itself to the roster when the United States Geological Survey, better known as the USGS, came to town in 1963 under the guidance of Eugene M. Shoemaker. Shoemaker set up offices and began to work with Lowell Observatory and the Atmospheric Research Observatory at the college in planning the upcoming moon exploration.

For a brief period in 1963, an area about fifteen miles northeast of Flagstaff was transformed into the moon. USGS technicians, using maps of the moon, had recreated a moonscape in the black cinder hills, blowing out craters and rearranging the earth until it was a dead-ringer for the area where the astronauts would land. They also built a prototype of the Moon Rover, a vehicle that would be deployed on the surface of the moon when astronauts landed. Flagstaff watched with awe as nine of the top astronauts spent their days training at the site. By 1965, the USGS claimed a permanent site on the top of McMillan Mesa, where they continue to play a major role in the United States space program. And thanks to Percival Lowell and the many others who followed, Flagstaff can claim a spot of fame on the world-wide map of space exploration. ✹

ABOVE: *A rocket pack was field tested in August 1966. The demonstrator managed to stay airborne for 21 seconds but had a great deal of trouble controlling the device. The USGS officials who witnessed the test decided that the rocket was too unstable to be used on the moon.* RIGHT: *In June 1964, USGS scientists from Flagstaff tested a spacesuit at Sunset Crater's Bonito Lava Flow. The man is collecting a geological sample. These years of training and preparation came to a head on July 20, 1969, when the Apollo 11 Project succeeded in landing on the moon. Millions watched as Neil Armstrong and Buzz Aldrin made history. Flagstaff shared the limelight when CBS news featured the involvement of our USGS branch in a nationwide television broadcast.*

OPPOSITE: *The preparation of astronauts for a moon landing included driving a training vehicle over the moonscape created by the USGS. Local employees Dick Wiser (Sherry Mangum's father), Bill Tinnin, and Putty Mills built the Explorer, shown here with a trainee.*

Women students dressed in football gear ham it up for the camera as they engage in a mock game on the lawn in front of Old Main around 1920.

Northern Arizona University

ORTHERN ARIZONA UNIVERSITY WAS not always the highly-accredited thriving institution we have today. It began when Flagstaff requested that territorial legislature build a significant public institution in the community. The response was to award Flagstaff a reform school.

Work started on the reform school building in the fall of 1894, and within a few months, the walls were up and the roof was on. Then cost overruns exhausted construction money, and the taxpayers of Arizona were left with a useless building that had no doors or windows. There were efforts to turn it into something functional, which resulted in the 1897 passage of a bill funding the conversion of the building into an "insane asylum." In 1898, doors and windows were fitted into the shell of the building, but plans for the asylum did not come to fruition. Finally, in 1899, Flagstaff's leaders convinced the legislature to employ the building as the Northern Arizona Normal School (NANS).

RIGHT: *This modern shot of Old Main shows that it has been maintained in good condition and embellished with trees and other landscaping.*

LEFT: *This is the first graduating class of the Northern Arizona Normal School in 1903. Four students failed to show up for the picture.*

NANS offered two four-year programs. One program led to a teaching certificate and the second to a high school diploma. NANS opened its doors in September 1899 with two faculty members and twenty-three students.

Until 1923, Flagstaff school children attended Emerson School for grades 1-8, and then went to NANS for grades 9-12. This changed when Flagstaff High School was built at the head of Sitgreaves Street, opening for the fall term of 1923. The removal of grades 9-12 allowed NANS to shed its normal school limitations, and it became Northern Arizona State Teachers College. In 1929, it was renamed Arizona State Teachers College at Flagstaff.

During the Second World War, the military services took away so many young men that the college enrollment dropped from a healthy pre-war total of 535 to a sad 136, and it teetered on the brink of collapse. The college was saved when it landed a Navy V-12 program. The V-12 program gave a training course to military personnel and used campus dormitories, classrooms, and facilities, paying the college for use privileges.

In 1945, the small teachers college was finally empowered to grant bachelor's degrees in arts and sciences as well as master's degrees in education. With this improvement came another name change to Arizona State College (ASC). Postwar students returned in record numbers thanks to education subsidies under the GI Bill, and conditions returned to normal.

LEFT: *From the beginning, there has been a friendly relationship between the university and the local residents. In this 1956 photo, the Homecoming parade rolls eastward through the heart of downtown on Route 66 just west of Humphreys Street. The Homecoming King and Queen sat on top of the big logging wheels and were pulled by students instead of horses.*
ABOVE: *One of the key moments in the evolution of the institution that began as Northern Arizona Normal School occurred in 1966 when Arizona State College became Northern Arizona University. Here a road crew is taking down the old sign to replace it with the new.*

ASC grew slowly, with 1,396 students by 1958. In that year, the legislature decided that Arizona should have a School of Forestry; and since neither Tucson, home of the University of Arizona; nor Phoenix, home of Arizona State University, was situated in a forest, Flagstaff felt that it deserved the new school. A fierce fight followed, but ultimately, the school was awarded to Flagstaff.

In 1964, when the enrollment was 3,337, ASC backers launched a well-coordinated campaign for university status. They convinced the legislature that with the school's increase in students, upgrading of programs, improvement of faculty, and capable leadership, it was due. The governor signed the bill in November 1964 and the change in status took place on May 1, 1966.

As a university, the school was able to award doctorate degrees for the first time in its history. In addition, it expanded its curriculum, providing degrees in business administration, engineering, and other fields. This attracted many new students, which meant that new faculty was hired, and new classrooms and dormitories were built. Achieving university status gave a dramatic boost to the school and the town. Student enrollment was 4,000 in the year that the bill was signed, and it swelled to nearly 6,000 in its first year as a university with a corresponding increase in faculty and facilities. Ten years after becoming Northern Arizona University (NAU) the enrollment had risen to 10,000, and twenty years later it was 15,000 and climbing.

BOTTOM LEFT: *To reflect the importance of the lumber industry to Flagstaff, the college adopted the Lumberjack as its sports mascot. For years, there was a Lumberjack Café at the junction of Milton Road and Mike's Pike. The owners purchased a giant lumberjack statue to advertise the restaurant.* BOTTOM RIGHT: *When the Lumberjack Café closed, the owners donated the statue to NAU. It was given a fresh coat of paint, and now stands near the Walkup Skydome.*

The administration scrambled to deal with the influx of students and construction continued for years after NAU was created. As well as development of the existing campus, the entirely new South Campus was built to accommodate the growth. This period of ebullient expansion culminated in the completion of a structure that has become a Flagstaff landmark, the Walkup Skydome in 1977. This huge building has given Flagstaff the ability to host sports, entertainment, and cultural events.

In the 1980s, there was an extension of NAU's physical location into selected areas of the state, such as Yuma, as part of the Distance Learning Program. In the 1990s, virtual expansion by the web, TV, and satellite was added to provide complete statewide coverage. Today, NAU even has an electronic Worldwide Campus. These out-reach programs throughout NAU's service area have served to temper the growth of the traditional Flagstaff campus, leaving Flagstaff with a beautiful campus that is a vital part of the city.

NAU's benefits to Flagstaff are countless. It is the city's largest employer, and students, faculty, and visitors add a considerable amount of money to the economy. But the blessings are more than economic. NAU also enables the city to enjoy activities not usually obtainable in a place of its size, such as symphony orchestras, theater, fine art, dance, and sporting events. And there are bookstores, coffee houses, and galleries that would not be here but for the university. The foresight of Flagstaff's leadership in creating a school of higher learning in the community will continue to be a blessing. ✿

THE AUTOMOBILE

IN 1900, THE FIRST AUTOMOBILE APPEARED on the Flagstaff scene. It was temporarily on display by S. A. Faroat, who wanted to run an auto stage line from Flagstaff to the Grand Canyon. Unfortunately, his endeavor never got off the ground, but by 1904 when Mrs. F. W. Sisson purchased the first locally owned automobile, the residents of Flagstaff knew this new mode of transportation was here to stay.

By 1909, there were so many cars trying to use Arizona's outmoded wagon roads that the territorial legislature had to deal with the new reality. It proposed a new road system that would allow all of Arizona to be reached by major highways. Flagstaff was chosen as the northern hub of intersecting north-south and east-west highways. Construction of the north-south highway was postponed, but the east-west highway followed the Beale Wagon Road, and became the National Old Trails Highway, the predecessor of Route 66.

With major roadways under construction, tourism to and from Flagstaff increased significantly. In 1911, the first automobile trip was made from Flagstaff to West Fork, a favorite camping and fishing resort in Oak Creek Canyon. The road, which roughly followed the path of today's Highway 89A, crossed the creek eleven times and the trip took almost three hours each way. Nevertheless, people bore such hardships willingly and soon were driving everywhere, opening the scenic wonderland to the world. By 1923, so many people were coming across Arizona by auto that park rangers counted an astonishing 23,000 cars at the South Rim of the Grand Canyon.

Flagstaff took to the automobile quickly. By 1920, the approximate date of this picture, there were dozens of them in town.

In 1926, John W. Weatherford finished a project that had taken him ten years to build—The Weatherford Road, or as it was officially named, The San Francisco Mountain Scenic Boulevard. Seeing the potential for tourist dollars, Weatherford originally built this road that leads to the saddle between Agassiz and Humphreys Peaks as a toll road, and placed a toll house at the foot of the road about three miles north of town. But even though the road had much to offer, the Great Depression hit and it fell into disrepair and disuse. Remnants of the road have been converted into a hiking trail, and the toll house is now a small home.

Fortunately for Flagstaff, the Great Depression only postponed road construction. In the years that followed, the town began to enjoy the fruits of tourism to an even greater degree, as its scenic attractions were completely accessible by the new web of roads. Slowly, Flagstaff found ways to take advantage of the growing economic situation, and the automobile was there to lead the way into the future. ✺

TOP: *Even though the roads were rough, Flagstaff citizens drove out in all directions to see the natural wonders of the area in a new way. It wasn't easy, and drivers could expect at least one flat tire per day on an outing.* BOTTOM: *One of the favorite playgrounds for Flagstaff was Oak Creek Canyon. Until good auto roads were built, getting to West Fork took 4-5 hours by wagon, and then an arduous hike down a footpath to the creek. The early auto roads were a trial, but the three autos shown here have made it to the Thomas Hotel, later called Mayhews Lodge, at West Fork.*

WATER WOES

❖

FLAGSTAFF HAS BEEN CONCERNED WITH the region's water supply since its earliest days. The first source of water was Old Town Spring from which residents filled water buckets to take to their homes. Rain barrels to catch runoff were also common and many homes had wells. A few old-timers made a living by bringing water into town from springs and selling it by the barrel. These uncertain supplies made the growth of town difficult.

The solution was obvious to everyone—bring water down from the Peaks. But this was a costly solution requiring expensive labor, miles of pipeline, a reservoir, and a system of mains and hydrants. Private enterprise could not handle the task, so residents took up the cause to incorporate the town, which was accomplished in 1894. The new town was then able to sell municipal bonds in order to raise the funds. Finally in 1898, under the leadership of Mayor Julius Aubineau, enough bonds were sold and the waterworks built.

A few years later, Tim and Mike Riordan, owners of the Arizona Lumber & Timber Company, made a generous contribution toward improving the city's water problem. They had their mill workers build a dam in Clark's Valley, seven miles southeast of town. The work commenced late in 1904, and by the early summer of 1905, the dam was finished and a lake began to form behind it, creating a large body of water that provided a reservoir for town usage. It was also large enough for recreational purposes, and soon boats dotted the surface and fishermen tried their luck along its banks. Tim Riordan named the lake after his daughter, and Lake Mary became a Flagstaff institution.

Even with water from the Peaks and Lake Mary, Flagstaff's growing population needed new supplies. In 1926, the town took a major step when it built a large new reservoir on Schultz Pass Road, three miles north of town. The added supply of water took care of growth during the next few years.

The next move in the development of the Flagstaff water system was the creation of another lake, when the city built the Upper Lake Mary Dam in 1941. The project included pumps and pipelines to bring the lake's water into a new treatment plant on the Lake Mary Road, which is still in use.

By the '50s, Flagstaff was experiencing a growth boom and again needed more water. The city decided to try drilling a well at Woody Mountain, five miles southwest of town. The drilling was tough, going through layers of solid rock, but at the 1,200-foot level the bit finally punched through into water—lots of water. It took another couple of years to build the lines into town and integrate the new supply into the municipal system, but it was accomplished just in time, enabling Flagstaff to withstand a severe drought in 1956. Today, the Woody Mountain Well Field is the primary source of the city's water. ❖

ABOVE: *Building the first water pipeline down from the Peaks in 1898 was a tough proposition. Much of the work was done by hand or with animal power. In this shot, donkeys are hauling water pipe up the steep slopes. Some of this original pipeline can still be seen today.* LEFT: *Before the pipeline brought tap water to town, many residents got their water from these entrepreneurs. The cost was an outrageous dollar a barrel. Needless to say, bathing was infrequent.*

ABOVE: *In most years, a good snow cover caps the San Francisco Peaks, as seen here. When the snow melts, millions of gallons of water are produced. Some of it disappears, but enough of it can be tapped from springs and wells to supply the city.*

RIGHT: *Lower Lake Mary, shown here, was the only lake until the upper dam was built in 1941. As a result, it held much more water than it does now. This 1905 shot shows a variety of boats enjoying the lake.*

OPPOSITE: *One of the best-known movies with scenes from Flagstaff is the 1969 film* Easy Rider, *starring Peter Fonda, Jack Nicholson, and Dennis Hopper. In this classic image, Peter Fonda and Luke Askew pose north of town at Wupatki National Monument.*

RIGHT: *This close-up view of Lomaki Ruin at Wupatki shows the kind of scenic Western beauty that attracted Hollywood to Flagstaff.*

FLAGSTAFF IN THE MOVIES

IN 1914, PIONEER MOVIE MOGUL JESSE Lasky made a brief stopover in Flagstaff, which could have changed the small community forever. Western movies were becoming very popular, and Lasky's cinema crews in New Jersey were finding it ever harder to create the illusion of Western landscapes in their films. Lasky had planned a blockbuster Western called *The Squaw Man* and wanted to shoot it in the real West, thereby relocating his studios to a suitable Western location. Flagstaff was on his final list of locations, but in the end, he postponed making his decision until he had seen one more town—Hollywood.

Flagstaff obviously lost that battle, but it was not the end of its cinematic career. Flagstaff did finally appear in a Hollywood movie in 1919, when a cinema crew that included Tom Mix shot scenes for a Western called *Hearts and Saddles* at Lake Mary. Before long, producers were using northern Arizona's scenery in a multitude of films, some of the most notable being *Easy Rider* and *Forrest Gump.* ✱

THE MOTHER ROAD

❧

THE YEAR OF 1912 WAS A BIG YEAR FOR Arizona. Not only did Arizona become an official state, but also the National Old Trails Highway Association was formed with the intention of creating the first highway to stretch from Baltimore to Los Angeles. That year, Flagstaff saw the creation of a wonderful highway that would have lasting effects on the growing town.

By 1913, the National Old Trails Highway was bringing hundreds of motorists through Flagstaff, stopping for gas, food, and lodging. Flagstaff citizens began to realize the business potential of serving auto travelers and soon were opening service stations, cafes, motels, and campgrounds. The National Old Trails Highway was well-traveled and the number of users increased every year.

In 1926, federal officials adopted a new highway system using numbers instead of names. The National Old Trails Highway disappeared and was replaced by U. S. Highway 66, which ran from Chicago to Los Angeles. The name change didn't matter much to Flagstaff residents—what counted was that they were located on a major highway, and Highway 66 held big promise. Soon the fledgling road gained a national reputation as being the premier sightseeing and recreation highway, the road of choice for those headed to California, the nation's playground.

Then the Great Depression hit, and by 1931, Highway 66 traffic had slowed to a crawl. One way the government responded to the depression was to create jobs by allocating extra money to highway projects, and as a result, the route was greatly improved during the '30s, being fully paved across Arizona in 1937. The work included the construction of an underpass in Flagstaff, allowing Highway 66 to cross under the railroad tracks at Sitgreaves, or present-day Milton Road.

As the grim decade wore on, Flagstaff citizens became used to a sad sight—hundreds of cars slowly moving through town en route to California in search of a new start. This migration that was captured poignantly by John Steinbeck in his celebrated book, "The Grapes of Wrath," gave Highway 66 a new image as "the highway of hope."

Finally, after long years of depression and war, there was a new surge of travel and Highway 66 came into its glory days. Bobby Troup wrote his hit song, "Get Your Kicks on Route 66," and the highway, better known now as "Route 66," became a household word. For the next ten years, traffic on Route 66 through Flagstaff surged with an ever-increasing number of travelers.

By 1956, however, Route 66, like most of the nation's other highways, was becoming outdated. Newer, faster, and more powerful cars made the old highways dangerous and inadequate. Congress decided to modernize the highway system and passed the Federal Highway Act. Under this law, the nation would build a system of modern highways engineered for high-speed auto travel. The new superhighways would have divided lanes and controlled access and would bypass towns. In October 1968, road crews finally finished the I-40 work around Flagstaff, making it the first Arizona city on Route 66 to be bypassed. Travelers no longer had to come through town for gas or groceries, but fortunately, because Flagstaff was not solely based on tourism, the community survived and continued to prosper.

In 1992, the city council decided to honor Flagstaff's heritage by changing the name of parts of Santa Fe Avenue, Sitgreaves Street, and Milton Road back to Route 66. Now visitors coming through Flagstaff can still see Route 66 signs, evoking memories of the glory days of the Mother Road. ❖

ABOVE: *This parade of vintage cars echoes the early days of automobile travel when motorists drove through the heart of Flagstaff on Route 66.*

OPPOSITE: *One of the favorite roadside businesses along Route 66 was the Dean Eldredge Museum on the east side of town. Eldredge collected curiosities and was also a taxidermist. He built this eye-catching building to lure tourists in to see his curios and buy souvenirs. Unfortunately for Eldredge, the business failed and he moved out, leaving mounted animal heads all over the walls. The property was turned into a nightclub called the Museum Club, and the owner kept the heads for decoration, giving the place its nickname, The Zoo.*

GRAND CANYON

METEOR CRATER

OAK CREEK CANYON

SUNSET CRATER-WUPATKI

For years, Flagstaff advertised itself as The City of Seven Wonders, even though not all of the wonders were actually located in Flagstaff.

SAN FRANCISCO PEAKS

THE CITY OF SEVEN WONDERS

R EALIZING THE NATURAL AND HISTORIC wealth scattered around the Flagstaff region, community leaders decided to fight for the preservation of their sacred areas. The fight began in 1915, when residents applied for and were awarded National Monument status for Walnut Canyon. A second victory followed in 1919, when the Grand Canyon was upgraded from a National Monument to a National Park. The Canyon, which now fell under the jurisdiction of the National Park Service, was able to purchase private property all along the South Rim. This meant that the park service could forbid any new mining claims, curb future development, and preserve the natural beauty of the Canyon.

These significant improvements were the beginning of a series of such events that allowed the Chamber of Commerce to call Flagstaff "the City of Seven Wonders." And even though some of theses wonders are outside of the immediate region and privately owned, Flagstaff representatives have been instrumental in their preservation.

MONTEZUMA'S CASTLE

WALNUT CANYON

LEFT: *New technology meets the old in this 1919 photograph. The first airplane that came to Flagstaff had such a puny engine that it was no match for Flagstaff's elevation. It taxied around and around the big field, but the airplane never left the ground. The embarrassed owners had to ship it back out by rail the same way it came in.*

RIGHT: *As airplanes improved they became part of the Flagstaff landscape. This terminal at Pulliam Field served until 1993 when it was replaced by larger and more modern facilities.*

AIRBORNE

❖

B Y THE EARLY 1900S, FLAGSTAFF WAS USED to the train whistle pulling into the station, as well as the sputtering of the car engine as it made its way down the main street, but airplanes were completely new. Flagstaff residents first saw an airplane in 1919, when promoters decided to make a stop-over in town. They proudly shipped the plane in by rail, loaded it onto a truck, and took it to the Babbitt pasture near present-day Museum of Northern Arizona. A large, amused crowd gathered to see this spectacular event. They watched with growing anticipation that shaded into concern and finally ended in laughter as the embarrassed pilot taxied endlessly around the pasture trying to get the machine into the air. Instead of flying triumphantly to its next stop, the plane had to be hauled out by train.

It was eventually understood that the first plane could not handle the high Flagstaff elevation. This was over-come in 1922, when promoters returned with a more powerful plane, and were able to fly successfully in and out of the Babbitt pasture.

In 1928, Flagstaff accepted the new form of transportation and built its first airport eight miles northeast of town in present-day Doney Park. It was named Koch Field in honor of I. B. Koch, Flagstaff's mayor.

By 1948, the city decided to build a new airport to replace the outmoded Koch field. When Pulliam Field was completed in 1949, Flagstaff became connected to the rest of the world by regular air service. This location has been used as an airport ever since that time, but the facility was improved significantly in 1993. In connection with the new terminal, an airport industrial park was designed and new safety and storage facilities were built. This new construction brought Flagstaff's airport up to modern-day standards. ❖

TELEVISION ARRIVES

✻

BECAUSE OF FLAGSTAFF'S SMALL-TOWN status, it was a little slow to get some of the modern conveniences that were showing up in larger cities. But in the '50s, Flagstaff finally saw a new kind of entertainment that had long been available to residents of Phoenix—television. The early TV sets were not very powerful and the stations had a limited broadcasting range. As a result, Flagstaff residents saw as much snow as programming at first. The Babbitts tried to remedy the situation with a closed-circuit subscription service, but its limited entertainment menu had so little appeal that it was dropped. Soon technology came to Flagstaff's rescue with improved sets and service, and by 1955, Flagstaff residents were just as addicted to the national programs like I Love Lucy and Sergeant Bilko as the rest of America. ✦

LEFT: *Flagstaff was behind the rest of the nation in getting television. By the mid-1950s, however, local stores were selling spiffy new console sets like the ones displayed in this photo.* ABOVE: *A few years after the arrival of television, Flagstaff had grown so much that it even had its own television studio.*

OPPOSITE TOP: *The Sechrist hospital only had 25 beds, but it served the community well for 20 years, occupying a small bit of land on the northwest side of Beaver Street.* OPPOSITE BOTTOM: *Today's sprawling medical center contains equipment and facilities undreamed of by earlier physicians. The skybridge connects the east and west campuses and symbolizes the value and importance of the hospital to the Flagstaff community.*

FLAGSTAFF'S MEDICAL HISTORY

I N 1955, THE TOWN GOT ITS FIRST PUBLICLY-
owned hospital when Dr. Charles Sechrist
donated the 25-bed facility, originally built in
1935. The hospital was thereafter managed on a not-for-
profit basis by a volunteer board of trustees. The hospital grew constantly over the years, entering a phase of
explosive growth in the 1980s and earning the name the
Flagstaff Medical Center. A Master Site Plan was created,
launching a long-term building program that is due for
completion in 2004. As a result of the construction that
has already taken place, the facility now covers the top
of Beaver Street and has made Flagstaff the regional
medical headquarters for northern Arizona. Over 67,000
patients visit the facility annually, 60 percent of them
coming from outside Flagstaff. There are over 160 doc-
tors on staff, and the center is one of Flagstaff's largest
employers with over 1,600 workers. In an era when
health care is one of the nation's primary concerns,
Flagstaff can be grateful for the generosity of the
Sechrist family and the foresight of the trustees.

ABOVE: *The city of Flagstaff and various business owners found that postcard advertising was cheap and effective. The cards they produced gave a picture of the town as it evolved over the years. The "Greetings from Flagstaff" card is interesting because it shows glimpses of Flagstaff in the cutout letters. Recognizable images are those of Old Main at NAU, the Monte Vista Hotel, and the Flagstaff Depot.*

OPPOSITE: *On the postcards seen here, the heart of the historic business district on Route 66 is presented. These images, which range from the early 1930s to the 1970s, offer the distinct impression that Flagstaff was still a rough and tumble frontier town. Old local favorites such as the Black Cat Café and Club 66 can be seen along the main route, and the Commercial Hotel, which was built in 1900 and burned down in 1975, is represented prominently in all of the postcards. Much of Flagstaff's face has changed since that time, but notice the Grand Canyon Café in the top right corner, which even today pays homage to the glory days of Flagstaff's past.*

Flagstaff, Arizona

HIGHWAY 66 THROUGH FLAGSTAFF, ARIZONA

STREET SCENE,
FLAGSTAFF, ARIZONA

BOTTOM: *The groundbreaking ceremony for the construction of the new community hotel was held in May of 1926.* LEFT: *The finished hotel became a downtown fixture, shown here in its prime around 1946.*

OPPOSITE: *Today, the hotel retains its looks and importance to Flagstaff's history. Notice the direction of the cars in the two finished hotel photos. Since this photo was taken, one-way streets have replaced most of the original two-way streets to promote traffic flow.*

THE MONTE VISTA

G OING WITH THE MID-DECADE PROSPERITY, city leaders decided that a new downtown hotel was needed, and in 1926, they organized the Flagstaff Community Hotel Corporation. In a whirlwind stock-selling campaign, they raised $200,000 and set out to build the hotel on prime downtown lots. They managed the project well, finishing it ahead of schedule and under budget, topping off the affair with a name-the-hotel contest. The winning entry was The Monte Vista, meaning "mountain view" in Spanish. Opening ceremonies took place on January 1, 1927, and the hotel was, and still is, a hit.

A few years later, Flagstaff got a second CCC camp at the base of Mt. Elden, and with this additional help, the visitor centers at Walnut Canyon, Wupatki, and Sunset Crater were built, together with the roads and parking lots needed to serve them. The men stabilized the ruins at Wupatki and built rangers' residences, utility buildings, and trails. Overall, the two groups of young men were priceless additions to the community. ✦

LEFT: *One of the beneficiaries of the work of the CCC was the Arizona Snowbowl. A fashionable early-day skier decorates the newly created slopes with her St. Bernard.*

CIVILIAN CONSERVATION CORPS AND THE ARIZONA SNOWBOWL

✦

ONE OF PRESIDENT ROOSEVELT'S Depression-era programs was the Civilian Conservation Corps, popularly called the CCC. Its goal was to create half a million jobs by recruiting young men, who were organized into military-style camps and paid for performing community projects. Flagstaff was lucky enough to land one of these camps in 1933.

Located in the Schultz Pass area, the camp contained two hundred young men who went to work on a large number of valuable projects. They realigned the Schultz Pass Road, created the Arizona Snowbowl and built the road leading to it, built a clubhouse at the golf course, and constructed a tree nursery. They built miles of fence, strung power lines, planted pine seedlings by the thousand, fought fires, built new forest roads and improved existing ones, hunted for lost hikers, built campgrounds, created ponds and tanks, and developed wells.

ABOVE LEFT: *In 1986, Snowbowl replaced the old Agassiz chairlift, which was by that time quite outdated, with a new and improved triple chair. Suddenly, Snowbowl's reputation as a modern ski area spread, and outdoor enthusiasts started arriving from all over the West. Since 1992, the ambitious endeavors of the new*

owners have resulted in the expansion of Hart Prairie Lodge, the creation of new trails, and the development of plans to expand the ski area. ABOVE RIGHT: *Snowbowl started operating in 1938 with just one small rope tow powered by a car engine. In 1962, the Agassiz chairlift was installed, allowing skiers to reach the top at a much improved pace.*

ABOVE LEFT AND RIGHT: *The Arizona Snowbowl
welcomes all kinds on mountain sports such as
downhill skiing, telemark skiing, and snowboard-
ing. The mountain has an expansive backcountry
area as well as a groomed snowboard park.*

RIGHT: *The Museum of Northern Arizona (MNA) was turned into a successful institution by transplanted Philadelphians Harold and Mary-Russell Ferrell Colton, shown with their son J. Ferrell.*
ABOVE: *By 1936, Mary-Russell had donated land for a museum campus and Harold had built the Exhibit Hall.*

OPPOSITE: *The Exhibit Hall has hosted countless exhibitions such as Exploring the Colorado Plateau and Histories in Clay, as well as cultural events, including the Hispanic Marketplace, the Hopi Marketplace, and the Navajo Show—which typically offered a beautiful display of intricately woven rugs.*

I N APRIL 1926, HAROLD AND MARY-Russell Ferrell Colton moved to Flagstaff. As wealthy Philadelphians, they had visited Flagstaff many times before deciding to move here, and during their visits they had helped fund the Museum of Northern Arizona.

In 1927, the Coltons led a campaign to revitalize their beloved museum, devoting their talents, energy, and money to it. With his scientific prowess (he had a Ph.D. in zoology) and her artistic talent (she was an academy-trained painter of note), the pair was perfectly matched to the new institution. His scientific curiosity reached out all over northern Arizona, delving into its geology, biology, botany, and archaeology. He studied the zoology of the area, trained himself in new fields such as volcanology and anthropology, and hired staff members to handle areas outside his knowledge. Mr. Colton insisted that he and his staff publish, and soon news of their work became widely known. Mrs. Colton taught art, sponsored art exhibits, and devoted herself to the improvement of the condition of Native American artists. Because of the Coltons' generous support, the Museum of Northern Arizona became a world-class institution. ✤

THE POW-WOW

IN 1930, A COLORFUL TRADITION BEGAN in Flagstaff—the Southwest All-Indian Pow-Wow. This event, centered around the Fourth of July, featured rodeos, parades, authentic ceremonials, and the sale of arts and crafts. It caught on with Native Americans and attracted members of tribes from all over America, who poured into Flagstaff every July. The organizers, a group of volunteer business and professional leaders, gave the celebration a national reputation with skillful advertising and promotion.

It was Flagstaff's primary festival, but the size of the crowds (up to 100,000) became increasingly unmanageable for the volunteer committee in charge of the event. However, they kept up their efforts until 1972, when an incident occurred that changed the future of the festival forever. Radical activists appeared at the celebration and disrupted the proceedings, claiming that the Pow-Wow exploited Native Americans. The committee tried to appease the protestors and when that failed they cancelled the remainder of the program. The following year, there were not enough sponsors to host the festival, and it was cancelled. For the next few years, several attempts were made to reestablish the Pow-Wow but nothing worked. Finally, in 1980, Flagstaff decided to cancel the Pow-Wow permanently. But even without the festival, local residents have found other ways to celebrate the Native American culture that continues to enrich Flagstaff. ❖

OPPOSITE TOP AND BOTTOM: *Citizens and visitors alike drank in the sights of the Pow-Wow, which was first held over the Fourth of July in 1930. This festival was such a success that it became an annual celebration for the next fifty years. One of the main events during the Pow-Wow was the daily noontime parade. The famous Hopi Indian Band always provided fast-paced music to accompany the parade participants, who were decked out in their traditional regalia.*

TOP: *After the daily parade, there was an all-Indian rodeo. In addition to the prize saddles donated by Doc Williams' Saddle Shop, cash prizes up to $50,000 were awarded to the winners.*
BOTTOM: *Beginning at dusk every night, ceremonial dances were held at the grandstands. Spectators would witness a variety of dances from the Hopi Rainbow Dance to the Arapaho Hummingbird Dance.*

I T WOULD SEEM THAT IF A TOWN WERE named after a flag staff, the people living there would know where it had originally been located. But that is not the case with Flagstaff, Arizona. "Everyone" knew where the staff had been—until someone tried to pin it down for historical accuracy. When it became an issue in the years after the town was named, it seemed that the old-timers could not agree at all, and a rather comic debate about the location of the staff ran on for years.

Newspaper mentions began to pop up in the years between 1910-1920. Some of these were little articles and others were letters to the editor from pioneers, who claimed to have been to Flagstaff in the old days and to have personal knowledge of the location of the staff. Unfortunately, those eyewitness accounts disagreed with each other. In the 1920s and 30s, as the earliest generation of pioneers began to die out, there were more letters to the paper seeking to nail down the original location of the staff. Again, there was no agreement.

In 1942, the Flagstaff Chamber of Commerce, at the behest of Harold S. Colton, Director of the Museum of Northern Arizona, decided that the time had come to gather all of the oldest citizens into a committee to decide once and for all where the staff had been located. Although many locations were bandied about, these true pioneers narrowed the locations down to three respectable contenders. One was Old Town Spring on Lower Coconino Avenue, another was Antelope Spring on Thorpe Road, and the third was a site just north of the railroad tracks east of Elden Street. After debating over the choices, the committee members agreed on the third site.

During the years that followed, additional evidence concerning the location of the staff came to light. In 1985, an evaluation of the new evidence led the members of the Flagstaff Historic Sites Commission to agree that the 1942 committee had been wrong. They determined that the site was at Antelope Spring on Thorpe Road just west of Marshall School. A monument featuring a tall flag staff with memorial plaques surrounding its base currently stands in that location. ❖

OPPOSITE: *This modern flag staff with the patriotic jet streaking the sky above is located at the Flagstaff Monument, which is on Thorpe Road near Marshall Elementary School. The monument honors the July 4, 1876 flag-raising ceremony that gave Flagstaff its name.*

RIGHT: *In 1942, the Flagstaff Chamber of Commerce created a committee of pioneers to locate the site of the original flag staff. Two of the members, William Switzer and George Hochderffer, are standing at the chosen site just east of Elden Street in downtown Flagstaff. Later evidence revealed that they were wrong about this site.*

WWII AND THE NAVAJO ORDNANCE DEPOT

❋

THE FORTIES ARE REMEMBERED AS THE war years, but the war didn't really hit Flagstaff until February, 1942 when the Army revealed that it was going to build a large munitions facility, the Navajo Ordnance Depot, in Bellemont, some ten miles west of Flagstaff. Federal officials wanted a large tract of land that would be easy to develop with water and railroad access near the West Coast but not so close as to be a target for submarines. Construction of the depot flooded Flagstaff with 15,000 workers and their families in a boom-town scenario not seen since the exhilarating days of railroad construction. Months later, after the construction was finished, a staff of 2,000 depot workers was hired, providing high-wage jobs aplenty.

America mobilized for war on an unprecedented scale and soon the conflict had an impact on every phase of life. Wartime conditions included rationing. Such staple items as meat, sugar, butter, and shoes were assigned points. To buy a pound of butter, for instance, might cost fifty cents and two points. Flagstaff citizens planted Victory Gardens in order to put fresh unrationed produce on the table. All over the country, financing the war was a major concern, and Flagstaff's citizens responded with Victory Bond drives and other fundraising activities so heartily that they had the best per capita record in the state for contributions.

Small white Service Flags began to appear in the windows of Flagstaff homes. These were sent by the military to the mothers and wives of servicemen. In the center of each flag was a blue star for each family member in uniform. Citizens learned to walk quietly and with respect past homes that added an additional star to the flag, a gold one, for this meant death. There were seventeen Gold Star Mothers in Flagstaff.

The war ended in 1945, and grateful residents whipped up an impromptu victory parade led by the town fire engine. After the war, in 1946, residents were relieved to hear that the Navajo Ordnance Depot would stay open, storing new munitions and disposing of returned and outdated ones. Though there would not be as many jobs there as there had been during the war, the base would continue to be a major employer. Old explosives had to be blown up for safety's sake, and for years after the war, Flagstaff citizens set their watches at noon when they heard the deep resonating booms of detonated munitions at the Depot. ❖

ABOVE: *This monument to the Flagstaff citizens who died while fighting for their country was dedicated on Memorial Day, 1990. It is located in Wheeler Park. Inscriptions on the stone pillar list each war and the names of Flagstaff's beloved who died in them. The Spanish-American War claimed one local life; World War I claimed nine; World War II, seventeen; Korean War, two; Vietnam, twenty-one. As this book was being written, more of Flagstaff's sons and daughters are dying in the Iraq War.* BELOW: *These guarded gates are what hundreds of employees saw every morning when they went to work at the Navajo Ordnance Depot during the height of World War II.*

TOP RIGHT: *Unprecedented numbers of Flagstaff men served in the military during World War II, such as Superior Court Judge H. Karl Mangum, who volunteered for the Navy in 1944. He is shown here in uniform with his son, author Richard Mangum, during his training at the Great Lakes Naval Base in Illinois. He and dozens of other local residents saw the world, broke through their provincial shells, and made Flagstaff a more enlightened, tolerant, and sophisticated town when they returned.* BELOW: *During the years of World War II, the war effort dominated the lives of citizens. The cost of the war was enormous, so the government was constantly urging citizens to buy war bonds and periodically another appeal would be made. Local Flagstaff businesses like the Orpheum Theatre always responded nobly by hosting events to help raise money.* LEFT: *Another way the Orpheum helped the war cause was to donate the proceeds of the ticket office on designated war bond movie nights.*

OPPOSITE: *Flagstaff was the railhead for the Glen Canyon Dam construction project. While underway, everything was done on a massive scale, especially the pouring of tons of concrete.*

BOTTOM: *The first bucket of concrete was poured on June 17, 1960, and after three years of hard work, the last bucket of concrete was poured and the dam was complete.* RIGHT: *The creation of the enormous dam resulted in Lake Powell, now a popular vacation destination.*

GLEN CANYON DAM

THE FIFTIES WERE A TIME OF FLOURISHING prosperity, and there was grand-scale construction in the air. In 1956, Congress appropriated $421 million dollars to build a dam across the Colorado River in Glen Canyon. This meant shipping in huge quantities of supplies, the preferred method being by rail. Flagstaff was the nearest town located on a railroad and became the headquarters for the project. A 300-acre industrial park was set aside for the construction depot four miles northeast of town, where the Flagstaff Mall is today, and the town of Page was created at the building site. For months materials rolled into Flagstaff on the train and were transferred onto trucks to be taken to Page. The huge project lasted for years and gave a golden boost to Flagstaff's economy.

Finally, in 1963 the last bucket of cement was poured and the trapped waters of the Colorado River slowly began to form Lake Powell. It wasn't long before boaters discovered the beauty of the lake's coves and inlets, and it became a premier recreation spot. Flagstaff quickly picked up on this new form of tourist traffic and easily adapted itself to the role of host once again. ❈

Today, Flagstaff golfers enjoy top quality courses, a far cry from the original dirt course that introduced an earlier generation to the game.

THE GOOD LIFE

❖

S INCE 1925, FLAGSTAFF GOLFERS HAD practiced their sport with grim forbearance on a nine-hole dirt golf course three miles north of town. There was no grass on the fairways or the greens. Finally, in the fifties, Flagstaff's growing prosperity triggered the construction of a new 18-hole grass course four miles east of town. It opened for play in 1959, and in time, it became the Continental Country Club, which is open to the public.

The subdivision lots lining the fairways of the golf course were sold and the owners began to build homes. There were a handful of homes there by 1975, but by the end of the decade, there were hundreds, and the east section of town began to take on a new tone. Local people decided that it was a favorable place to live and overcame their previous reluctance to move from the center of town.

The next step up in luxury arrived when the Forest Highlands subdivision started construction in 1987. Up to this time, Flagstaff had enjoyed some status as a summer playground for sweltering Phoenix citizens, but the Highlands was different. As a gated-community it clearly served the affluent, who did not have to make a living here. The project was successful and Flagstaff took on another aspect, that of a second-home vacation resort, catering to wealthy out-of-towners who paid premium prices to enjoy the mountains, clean cool air, golf, and country club living conditions. Today, more gated communities are being added to the area, and Flagstaff continues to grow in affluence and luxury. ✺

THE FLAGSTAFF ZOO

ABOVE: *McMillan Mesa, where Flagstaff's living zoo was located in the early '60s, is an area of natural beauty. The zoo was given the name Buffalo Park, and it was home to ducks, elk, and an entire herd of buffalo, seen here in the distance.* BELOW: *While the stagecoach ride through Buffalo Park delighted the visitors, there weren't enough of them to keep the park in business. After the park's closure in 1969, the city decided to designate the land as a public park and kept the original name in honor of the Buffalo that once populated the living zoo.*

FLAGSTAFF FLOURISHED IN THE FIFTIES, and its construction boom progressed at a steady rate well into the early 1960s, when the town was ready to build something new—a living zoo. In 1963, a site was picked out on McMillan Mesa just north of Cedar Road, and Buffalo Park was created. It featured a small lake stocked with ducks and other waterfowl; a few native animals such as elk; and the main attraction, a herd of buffalo. A stagecoach took visitors through the park, where they could see the gentle buffalo grazing. The park was intended to pay its own way through admission fees, but unfortunately, it didn't take in enough revenue and had to close in 1969. The land where it stood, complete with a bronze buffalo statue, is now a crown jewel of the city's park system, heavily used by a generation of citizens who walk its paths and wonder how it got its name.

1972

1978

THE CENSUS

❖

THE FIRST PUBLIC CENSUS taken in Flagstaff occurred in the year 1900. At that time, population counts were also taken in Holbrook, Winslow, Williams, and Kingman, all of which were along the path of the Atlantic & Pacific Railroad. The population numbers recorded that first year show that the towns were roughly matched with Holbrook at 256; Winslow at 1,305; Flagstaff at 1,271; Williams at 1,207; and Kingman at 651.

By 1950, all of the towns along the railroad had increased in size. However, Flagstaff was slowly pulling out in front of the rest. In the 1950 census, the following population figures were recorded: Holbrook, 2,336; Winslow, 6,518; Flagstaff, 7,663; Williams, 2,152; and Kingman, 3,342.

By the 2000 census, Flagstaff was definitely the leading city in northern Arizona. Year 2000 figures show Holbrook at 4,917; Winslow at 9,250; Flagstaff at 52,894; Williams at 2,842; and Kingman at 20,069. ❖

1988

1998

The shape of Flagstaff has always had a distinct footprint, and this series of aerial photographs shows how the town has developed over a period of twenty-six years.

LEFT TO RIGHT: In **1972**, Flagstaff had a population of 28,000, and a few communities were firmly established including downtown, Coconino Estates just northwest of downtown, and Bow and Arrow on the south side off Lake Mary Road. In **1978**, the population increased to 33,000, and suddenly homes started to appear in Cheshire, located northwest on Highway 180, University Heights, which is just south of I-40 and west of I-17, and Country Club, seen nestled around the golf course on the east

side of town. During this time period, the road over Cedar Hill also expanded, which helped East Flagstaff start to develop and prosper. Ten years later in **1988**, Flagstaff's population reached 43,600, and the family-friendly neighborhood of Cheshire has filled out, the Walmart complex suddenly appears on the map just north of I-40, and the Woodlands Village area on Old Route 66 now contains a large number of growing businesses and homes. Finally, in **1998**, the population has grown to 53,000, and there are few undeveloped areas in Flagstaff's original footprint. New areas that can be seen are Doney Park on the easternmost side of town and Boulder Point, located south of the Woodlands Village community.

NEW INDUSTRY

IKE OTHER TOWNS IN NORTHERN Arizona, Flagstaff was looking to attract new industries that adhered to the city's environmental, water-wise standards. The town found a perfect match, and in 1966, W. L. Gore opened for business.

The owners, who lived in Delaware, wanted to relocate to the West, and had spent years scouting out the perfect location. When they came to Flagstaff, they knew they had found their new home. The Gore operations expanded into ten plants, employing over one thousand workers by 1990.

Gore opened up the doors to new environmentally-friendly industries that Flagstaff wanted to attract. The next industry to fit that mold was Ralston-Purina, which came in 1975 and constructed a plant five miles east of town. Today, these two industries still rank among the top Flagstaff employers.

LEFT AND ABOVE: *Flagstaff's original industry, the lumber mill, was smoky, noisy, and dangerous. Modern industries, such as W. L. Gore, are not only quiet, smokeless, and safe, but also beautiful.*

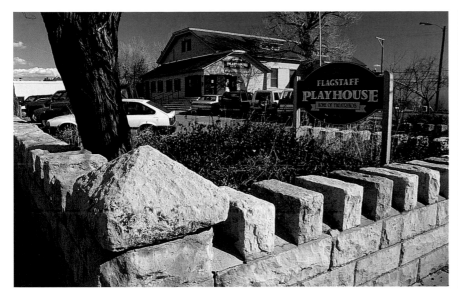

THE PUBLIC LIBRARY

TOP LEFT: *The Flagstaff Public Library was located for many years on the site of the C. J. Babbitt home (see page ix). It moved in 1987, and the building was taken over by Theatrikos, Flagstaff's premier theatre.* TOP RIGHT: *The new library is well loved and constantly busy, a far cry from its previous existence.*

E VEN IN ITS EARLY DAYS, FLAGSTAFF SAW the need for a library. The first try came in 1884 in the form of a public reading room. Unfortunately, it was located in a saloon, which made it inaccessible to the majority of residents. A few years later, growing interest led to the formation of the Flagstaff Literary Society, which sponsored the first official public library. But tragedy struck during a 1893 fire, and all the books were lost.

In 1914, under the leadership of the Flagstaff Woman's Club, a new library was created. It was located in the upstairs section of the Sanderson Building at 11 E. Aspen Avenue. By 1938, the City of Flagstaff assumed responsibility for the library and purchased the Woman's Club building at 212 W. Aspen Avenue, where it was housed for many years.

By 1972, the city's population had grown so large that the Women's Club building was no longer adequate. The city's first thought was to expand and enlarge the building, but inspectors examined it and immediately pronounced that it was not only unfit for expansion but was unsafe and had to be vacated immediately. To build a new library from scratch seemed financially impossible at the time, so the city bought the old Union Hall building on the southeast corner of Beaver Street and Cherry Avenue and remodeled it for library use, opening it in 1972. But from the beginning, the library was cramped for space in the Union Hall building, and as the years passed it became more and more inadequate. By the 1980s, it had sprouted leaks and was an eyesore.

Citizens began to urge the construction of a brand new public library. The matter was studied and city property west of Wheeler Park was chosen as the site. The new building was the first in Flagstaff's history to be designed as a library from the ground up. The result was a sparkling new structure that opened its doors to the public in May 1987. It was so attractive that readership increased three-fold within a few weeks. It fit beautifully into the City Hall-Wheeler Park complex and gave the city a proud new look. A further boon from the library construction was that the Union Hall building was available for other community use, so it became the home of Theatrikos, an amateur acting troupe that presents live plays, adding another feather to Flagstaff's cultural cap. ✖

FLAGSTAFF, AT ITS ELEVATION OF 7,000 feet, has had more than its share of big snowfalls. Two of the biggest in the Twentieth Century were in the winters of 1915-1916 and 1948-49. But, the winter of 1967 also had a surprise up its sleeve for the bustling town. In the second week of December, snow started to fall and kept coming down so heavily that 68 inches accumulated within a few days. Hardly had this been plowed away when another storm hit. Before the winter was over, 150 inches had blanketed Flagstaff. Roofs collapsed, roads were closed, and people in outlying areas were stranded. It was a reminder to Flagstaff citizens that Mother Nature was still in command.

Flagstaff had something else to worry about in 1972. That winter, continuing over into the early months of 1973, the city had its largest snowfall on record. But unlike the big snows earlier in the century, this snowfall was spread out over a longer time period, so removal crews were able to get the streets open before the next storm hit. That year, Flagstaff saw a total of 210 inches of fresh, white snow. ❄

OPPOSITE: *Trying to clear Aspen Avenue during the 1915-16 storm with horse-drawn plows was a difficult proposition.*

ABOVE: *During the winter of 1948-49, the Withers family was barely able to shovel away enough snow to get to their front door at 819 W. Aspen Street.* RIGHT: *During that same winter, there was so much snow that cars could not handle the streets.*

OPPOSITE: *The Church of the Nativity at the northeast corner of Beaver and Cherry has been a Flagstaff landmark since 1929, and it has seen more than its share of big snowfalls. In past years, Flagstaff's plows were able to clear the streets for cars, but the sidewalks often remained impassable.*

RIGHT: *The same shot taken years later shows that despite the rough winters, this charming building has remained strong and sturdy.*

LEFT: *Bruce Babbitt was a sophomore at Flagstaff High School when this yearbook picture was taken in 1953. Those who knew him then expected great things from him, and he did not disappoint them. After graduating from Flagstaff High School in 1956, he earned a bachelor's degree in geology from Notre Dame, where he was student body president. He followed this with a master's degree in geophysics from the University of Newcastle, England, and he finished his education with a law degree from Harvard.* ABOVE: *Bruce Babbitt became Arizona's Attorney General in 1975, and its governor in 1978. His inauguration ceremony, shown here, took place on March 4, 1978 at the Arizona State Capitol. Babbitt went on to become one of the best governors Arizona ever had, serving from 1978 to 1987. In 1993, he was appointed Secretary of the Interior by President Clinton and served in that office during all eight years of the Clinton Administration.*

Sophomores

tters
ent
offman
g
cative

Richard Anderson
Frank Avelar
Frank Auza
Bruce Babbitt
Ernestine Baca

Bonnie Baker
Elizabeth Barden
Carol Baseman
Billye Blair
Wanda Blem

Nancy Books
Cora Mae Boswell
Mathew Boyd
Nancy Bradshaw
Don Brinton

Frankie Byrom
Mary Ceballos
Delores Chavira
Ralph Chavira
Nancy Chiappetti

LAGSTAFF NATIVE BRUCE BABBITT BECAME governor of Arizona in 1978 and served the state extremely well. Babbitt, who had earned a bachelor's degree in geology from Notre Dame, a master's degree in geophysics from the University of Newcastle in England, and a law degree from Harvard, was elected Arizona's Attorney General in 1974, learning the political ropes and earning a reputation as a brilliant and effective leader.

In 1978, Governor Raul Castro resigned, the Secretary of State—who was next in line—died, and by law Babbitt became governor. He spent some time analyzing the state's needs and surrounding himself with capable assistants. After deciding that the primary need was to secure the state's water resources and establish water rights with certainty, he pushed through new comprehensive groundwater laws that resolved critical water issues for the first time in Arizona's history. He was also a champion of health care and education and made many needed improvements in these vital areas. But through it all, he was a fiscal realist who realized that money had to be provided to pay for even the most beneficial programs. He came up with new revenue sources and won the respect of friend and foe alike for his willingness to hear all points of view. He was probably the most effective governor that Arizona ever had in his ability to persuade people to work together for the common good, putting aside personal and political differences. He was elected in 1982 for a four-year term, and finished his eight years of service held in the highest esteem. During his term of office, he attended a national governors' conference where he met the governor of Arkansas, little-known Bill Clinton, who was quick to recognize Babbitt's gifts.

In 1992, Bill Clinton was elected President, and when he put his cabinet together he remembered the bright young man he had met while both were governors in the 1980s. The result was that he appointed Flagstaff's Bruce Babbitt to be United States Secretary of the Interior. Babbitt remained in office throughout the eight years of the Clinton administration and established himself as an honest and dedicated public servant, who was keenly interested in environmental issues and worked tirelessly to advance them. ❖

BELOW: *After years of public service, Bruce Babbitt now works as a private consultant in Washington DC.*

When Coconino Community College first opened in 1991, it didn't have a campus and had to make do with a variety of rented spaces. After a few months of struggling with this awkward and inefficient arrangement, the school took over a shopping center in East Flagstaff and converted the shopping spaces into classrooms. This was a step up, but the converted strip mall was still not enough. College supporters began to plan for a campus that was specifically designed for their needs. The Lone Tree campus of the Coconino Community College, opened in 2002, was the result. In its beautiful and functional new location, the college prides itself on providing useful programs, caring instructors, affordable tuition, smaller classes, new high-tech equipment, and successful transfers to state universities.

COCONINO COMMUNITY COLLEGE

F LAGSTAFF'S ROLE AS NORTHERN ARIZONA'S educational center expanded when Coconino County Community College opened in 1991. The organizers wanted to make higher education available to residents who were unable to attend Northern Arizona University due to geographic and economic barriers.

The institution was first seen as a school without walls, teaching from an assortment of donated classrooms. Soon it saw the need for a physical base and began to convert a former shopping center on Fourth Street into a campus. Next, the growing college acquired space for branches in Page and Williams and came closer to its goal of reaching out to all residents of the county. Public response was warm and students poured in to take advantage of a wide variety of classes. In 1995, the name of the school was shortened to Coconino Community College (CCC), and in 1996, its solid academic standing was established when it gained accreditation.

Having accomplished much in its first five years, the school's supporters began to make plans for an official campus in Flagstaff. The financing of the ambitious project required a bond election, which was held in November 1997. County voters approved $25 million in bonds, and construction went ahead. The new Lone Tree campus opened in April 2002, and the spacious new facility was well received.

Overall, the growing college has been an outstanding success, and the average annual enrollment at the two Flagstaff campuses is 5,720, with Page adding 710 and Williams 93. Coconino Community College has truly carried out its original mission—to make higher education available and affordable to the northland. ❋

ABOVE: *Since 1996, the city of Flagstaff has set aside over 600 acres for public parks. To date, 29 of the approximate 60 parks have been completed. Included are large community parks to smaller, more specialized parks for skateboarding, walking dogs, and playing disc golf. The city has also completed over 25 of its projected 50-mile Flagstaff Urban Trail System. This system will provide city-wide recreation and alternate transportation for outdoor enthusiasts.* RIGHT: *Wheeler Park, located across from Flagstaff's City Hall, hosts numerous public events including Art in the Park, Earth Day, and musical festivals such as this Celtic Fair.*

MANY PEOPLE WHO LOVE FLAGSTAFF have chosen to live here because of its unparalleled offering of outdoor activities. The City of Flagstaff, responding to this widespread interest, has for years been expanding and improving its parks and other recreational outlets. In 1996, it officially supported this way of life by committing to a long-range master plan for the creation and preservation of its parks.

Under the master plan, residents now enjoy twenty-nine city parks, ranging from small pocket parks to large community parks, and more parks are slated for creation in the future. An effort has been made to have some kind of park in every section of the city so that all citizens may enjoy them. The city has even gone so far as to create public parks specifically designed for dog-lovers and skateboard fanatics.

As part of the city's Master Plan, residents were delighted to see Flagstaff's 1895-era playground, Thorpe Park, rejuvenated and upgraded. For decades it was an uncut diamond, scratched out of the native soil and decorated with a few swings. Today, it is a beautiful grass- covered park with modern playground and recreation equipment.

The city also has responded to the desires of the many residents who love to hike and bike by creating the Flagstaff Urban Trail System, or FUTS. Many of the trails, which are of superior quality, have been constructed, and in time, they will surround the town and radiate out into the forests. Coconino County also fell into step when it added a Trails Planner to its staff in 1999, who has already built trails to complement the city system. And in addition to the numerous trails offered by the city and county, the Forest Service maintains a wide-spread system of paths. In all, Flagstaff's ever-expanding system of trails and outdoor recreations facilities are appreciated and beloved by all outdoor enthusiasts. ✿

A   B   C   D

TOP: (A) *After half of the Babbitt building was torn down, citizens discussed how the empty property should be used. During the discussion phase, the empty lot was used as an unpaved public parking lot, as shown in this shot from 1994. Finally, the city accepted a plan to create Heritage Square.* (B) *The first part of the plan, which took place in 1997, required excavation work to be done on the dirt parking lot in order to create an underground parking facility.* (C) *In 1998, the underground facility was then roofed and ready for the square to be built.* (D) *The project was finally finished and dedicated in June 1999 with a public ceremony. It then became a venue for a wide variety of events, including this performance of the U.S. Navy Band in 2001.*

The space for Heritage Square became available in 1990. Citizens agreed that it was prime downtown real estate but disagreed about how it should be used. Five Flagstaff citizens—Dick and Jean Wilson, Jim Babbitt, Steve Vanlandingham, and Francis McAllister—championed the idea of using the property as a public square, something that Flagstaff had never had before. They formed the Heritage Square Trust to try to reach their goal, and in 1992, the city accepted their proposal. OPPOSITE BOTTOM AND ABOVE: *Today, the 18,500 square-foot area contains the Empress Amphitheater; brick and stone railroad tracks honoring Flagstaff's heritage; a variety of bronze plaques that feature Flagstaff's scientific history; various benches that pay homage to the Observatory, ranching, logging, and the town's Native American influences; a fountain flowing from a rock that represents Old Town Spring, and a flag staff commemorating Flagstaff's humble origins.*

 BEFORE THE SEVENTIES, FLAGSTAFF'S business district had always been located downtown. But that decade saw growth and progress in other areas of the city that began to pull people and businesses away from downtown. By the late 1970s, Flagstaff's historic downtown district was struggling to stay alive.

The first pull away from the town center occurred with the introduction of strip malls. A few businesses moved outwards, and slowly the departures began to mount up. When the Flagstaff Mall opened in 1980, many citizens were elated. This was Flagstaff's first large enclosed air-conditioned mall, and it brought new stores to town as well as drawing in Penney's and Sears from other locations. Shoppers were attracted to the mall by its novelty, promotions, and big parking areas. But the mall accelerated the flight of business away from the downtown district, and before long, it was a hollow shell.

Flagstaff's historic downtown district dragged into the Nineties looking sad and neglected. In 1990, several members of the Babbitt family decided to do something about the depressing situation. They repurchased the old Babbitt store building and set about remodeling it. Additions to the original 1888 building had been built in 1891 and 1904, with both of the later structures wrapping around the earlier structure in an L-shape. The portions of the building that extended west on Aspen Avenue were trimmed back to the depth of the original building, effectively cutting the building in half. Then the 1957 flat white façade was removed, revealing the old red sandstone and brick underneath. The project was an encouraging success, and the public response to the restoration was enthusiastic.

Another renovation soon to follow was the 1915 Babbitt Garage building at the southwest corner of Birch and San Francisco, which was purchased by the Aspey, Watkins, and Diesel law partners. They spent a considerable amount of money remodeling the building and restoring its original look. The result was a triumph, and for the first time in its history a federal courtroom was opened in Flagstaff on the second floor of the building.

The renewal of interest in the historic town center led to a major downtown improvement, which began in 1994. New sewer pipes and other underground improvements were installed, and above ground new sidewalks, benches, old-fashioned street lights, and signs were built or installed. This went hand-in-hand with the building renovation being done by property owners, and a new downtown emerged.

The downtown renaissance came to its peak in 1999. In January of that year, Henry and Sam Taylor, owners of the Weatherford Hotel, held a dedication ceremony to celebrate the restoration of the hotel's historic balcony, missing from the building since a 1929 fire caused its removal. The reconstruction of the balcony dressed up downtown once again. At the same time, work was nearing an end across the street on an area that for years had been an unkempt dirt parking lot. In June 1999, work on the parking lot conversion was complete and Heritage Square was open, giving Flagstaff a town center for the first time. In addition to a public square, the project included a commercial building and underground parking. The square has been immensely popular with young and old alike and is a welcome addition to Flagstaff's revitalized historic district. ❖

RIGHT: *The building at 16 E. Route 66 was originally constructed as a liquor store and served that purpose until Arizona adopted Prohibition in 1915. Its neighbor at 18 E. Route 66 is primarily remembered as being a newsstand and tobacco store. After Prohibition, the former liquor store became a saloon. It sold Arizona Brewing Company beer under the ABC brand name. In the late 1940s, the two properties were consolidated under the ownership of Jerry Andreatos, a restaurateur. He remodeled the newsstand into a restaurant, and he converted the liquor store into El Patio Lounge, covering up the ABC Beer sign as he remodeled. At that time, the Commercial Hotel stood on the lot to the west of El Patio. After fire destroyed the hotel in 1975, the empty lots on which it sat were vacant and gave Route 66 a raw, unfinished look. In 1979, Phyllis Hogan opened Winter Sun, a family-owned and operated business specializing in American Indian art and Southwest botanicals, in the 18 E. Route 66 location.* ABOVE: *Finally, in the early 1990s, many of the new business owners began to remodel Flagstaff's historic buildings. In 1994, the new owners of Flagstaff Brewing Company (FBC) stripped off the smooth stucco facing and exposed the old ABC brick façade underneath. In July of that year, they opened for business. Today, the owners of FBC have renovated much of the original look of the building, added a nice patio area, and turned the once empty lot where the Commercial Hotel stood into a relaxing venue to enjoy outdoor music.*

ABOVE: *Another grand restoration project that occurred in the 1990s was the removal of the 1957 facing from the Babbitt building. The old red sandstone that had been covered for 46 years was proudly revealed and the building regained its classic look.*

LEFT: *The wave of remodeling and renovation that swept downtown led to the relocation of several businesses. Winter Sun, which was previously located on E. Route 66, found a new home nestled in the east side of the beautifully restored Babbitt building. The Babbitt building now houses a variety of businesses, showing that Flagstaff's historic downtown district is alive, vital, and healthy once again.*

TOP LEFT: *When the Babbitt Garage was constructed at the southwest corner of San Francisco and Birch in 1915, it was one of the largest buildings in town. The garage moved in 1959, and a variety of retail stores occupied the building until 1990 when it sat vacant and began to deteriorate.*

BOTTOM LEFT: *The Aspey, Watkins, and Diesel law firm bought the building, and in 1992-1993 they renovated it, adding an elevator to the south side. The result was a masterpiece, a splendid building that houses the federal court, law offices, and retail shops.*

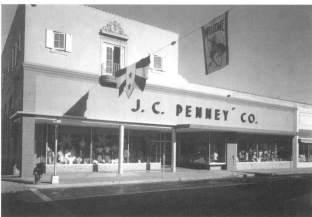

TOP RIGHT: *The Verkamp Building at the southeast corner of San Francisco and Aspen was built in 1899. The Elks Club occupied the upper story, and on the ground level was a drug store. The town's first bowling alley was located in the basement.* BOTTOM RIGHT: *In 1926, Fred Breen remodeled the building and added a veneer of new brick. Breen, who also owned the Coconino Sun, moved his newspaper offices into the building and rented the top floor as apartments. When he died in 1932, F. W. Moore purchased the property and painted the Moore Drug Co. sign on the north wall, which is still visible today. In the early 1970s, McGaugh's Newsstand took over the space, and they became a downtown fixture until their unfortunate closure in 2001.*

OPPOSITE TOP RIGHT: *In 1917, Flagstaff saw the arrival of its first chain store—J. C. Penney. It was originally located at 117 East Aspen, and then moved numerous times in the downtown area before finding a permanent home in the Flagstaff Mall in 1975. Other downtown locations included the Masonic Building, the Kinlani Building, and the corner of Leroux and Birch where the Old Town Shops are today.*
OPPOSITE BOTTOM RIGHT: *After Penney's moved out of the Kinlani building, a number of businesses occupied the location. Today, it is a popular downtown pub.*

OPPOSITE: *Located on "Knob Hill," this building was one of Flagstaff's finest homes, built in 1894 for pioneer E. S. Clark. He sold the home to banker T. E. Pollock in 1907, and Pollock made it a showplace for his new bride. After Pollock's death, the Souris family owned the property from 1943-1965, and they gave it good care.*

BELOW: *After 1965, the home went through a series of owners, including the Sigma Nu fraternity, during which time it fell into disrepair.*

RIGHT: *It was rescued and restored in 1989, and in 1991, it opened as an outstanding bed and breakfast known as The Inn at 410. In 2003, Gordon and Carol Watkins, both career veterans of the hospitality industry, purchased the business. Together with their son, Skylar, they look forward to welcoming their guests to "one of the most charming bed and breakfasts in all of Arizona."*

THE NEW MILLENNIUM

✽

NEW YEAR'S EVE, 1999, SAW THE beginning of a new Flagstaff tradition. Close to 2000 people gathered in Heritage Square to count down the remaining moments of 1999 and celebrate the coming of the new millennium. In similar fashion to the famous dropping of the ball at Times Square in New York City, the citizens of Flagstaff watched a six-foot lighted pine cone drop slowly from the top of the Weatherford Hotel. Now every New Year's Eve can be celebrated with friends and neighbors at this festive community event. ✽

A crowd of Flagstaff revelers greets the New Year at Heritage Square, watching the pine cone drop from the top of the Weatherford Hotel. Were they thinking about the 120 years of Flagstaff's past or just enjoying the present? This popular event has become an annual Flagstaff tradition.

THE PROMINENT AUTHOR/PHOTOGRAPHER TEAM of Richard and Sherry Mangum has played an active role in the Flagstaff community. In 1993, Richard, a Flagstaff native, and Sherry, a resident since 1958, originated the Flagstaff Historic Walk. This event has allowed the couple to share their love and knowledge with countless visitors. They have also produced nine books together including *Flagstaff Album, Route 66 Across Arizona, The Grand Canyon-Flagstaff Stage Coach Line, One Woman's West, The Hopi Silver Project, Flagstaff Hikes, Sedona Hikes, Williams Guidebook,* and *Flagstaff Historic Walk.* In recognition of their historic and literary efforts, they have been honored with the Copper Quill Award and named Flagstaff Ambassadors.